T0155138

JOSHUA TROTTER
MISSION CREE

Coach House Books, Toronto

first edition

Published with the generous assistance of the Canada Council for the Arts and the Ontario Arts Council. Coach House Books also acknowledges the support of the Government of Canada through the Canada Book Fund and the Government of Ontario through the Ontario Book Publishing Tax Credit.

LIBRARY AND ARCHIVES CANADA CATALOGUING IN PUBLICATION

Trotter, Joshua, author
        Mission creep / Joshua Trotter.

Poems.
Issued in print and electronic formats.
ISBN 978-1-55245-319-3 (paperback).

        I. Title.

PS8639.R657M57 2015   C811'.6   C2015-905040-5

Mission Creep is available as an ebook: ISBN 978 1 77056 428 2

Purchase of the print version of this book entitles you to a free digital copy. To claim your ebook of this title, please email sales@chbooks.com with proof of purchase or visit chbooks.com/digital. (Coach House Books reserves the right to terminate the free digital download offer at any time.)

For Ellie, Will and Luke

A Growing Group of Concerned Citizens   7

Sympathy for the Details   32

Some Evidence for Heightened Sexual Attraction under
Conditions of High Anxiety   54

Use of Tools   56

Fabulous Bird Periodically Burns Itself to Death, Rises
Afresh from the Ashes   66

Life Is Hard and Full of Miniseries   70

When the Great Wave Finally Reaches Your Town,
Who Will Warn You, and How?   71

Auto Parts, Shoes, Shorts, Cheerios   78

The Ghost Is Clear   80

I Know You Are But What I Am   85

Transmission Creep   87

In the Corporeal Manner to Which We Have Grown
Accustomed   89

When I asked The Oracle, Was there a here before I was born, she said, Oh dear, no dear, there was not. How lonely was the noun before the verb. The trees were black. The streets were black. The path I'm asking you to take is black, except this bleeding shaft of light laid out before us, which turns black too, at three or four feet. You'd think two of us would see more clearly, and three or more would light the map entirely, but you'd be off base, carousing with civilians. I need your mind as sharp as shattered mirror to help me trace the time and motion calculations. You will experience a distinct lack of emotion. Decreasing range of accountability. The dead will be uncounted. Histories will become few. I wanted to throw a complicated landing party, but I had nine, eight, seven microseconds with which to work. Ice receded like bathwater draining. There was a kind of spring, after months feigning. No criminal consciousness. No automatic compensation. No new aftermath. I can't count very high, but I try, scanning graffitied alleyways for ghosts of PalmPilots lost, wristwatches tossed, storied Sonys. I feel a hiccup in my lifestream every time I turn over a new leaflet. One's mined wonders. One's mind's reels. The sky is the colour of a drowned channel hopper's highland sweater. Let me be your cocaine carry-on. Your clarion luggage. Let me be your miracle Oracle, leaping twenty-seven burning school buses. Let THE BANALITY OF EVEL KNIEVEL be my mid-life mortality ploy, mired in the rubble of the theatre and its double. Let us learn to fall for the stuntman who takes the money and runs out of gas on the ramp. Let the Iron Wind gather voluble information from back alleys and cliffs. In the deluge, the river's visage grows stubble. The glacier-gouged harbour grows choppier. We're all here, sweating by the photocopier in the shadow of the Dome of Food or Pleasure, harvesting nuts and grubs from beneath seat cushions in the Gun Lobby. The difference between hunting for food and hunting for fun is one sandwich short of a picnic. The difference between copies makes copies perfect. Travel through space is travel through time's narrow hips, exiting an opening unsuitable for giving birth to big ideas. I have a Boeing 767 in my closet. Don't worry about the dearth of my species. I've been posting reproductions [unintelligible] over vast distances. The Iron Wind takes pointers from its cousin, cosine ocean, working 24–7 perfecting booty. The perfect body is no body. Perfect copy no copy. On shore leave, by shortwave <15 MHz>, inner child labourers loiter by goitered rivers, genuinely loving Champagne. Pay no attention to your own expression <27 MHz> eddying in the pool between your knees. Copy? The river slows and makes of you a special offer. You've won your own ignoble prize. Spilled your guts and made yourself a tool. Awkward. Wow. What now? Imagine hauling from your lost vomitus smaller seagulls scrapping and squalling, scouring the banks for tourists flinging haute cuisine. Cognitive dissidents, trained in the camps of letter carriers, seagulls are spry descendants of the spleen. Let us not forget the War Between the Things That Made Us Human. Back when red was rad, the feds were outraged, art-kids splattered every shade on their tattered Converses. Back then, certain measures saved prudent masters: plant no rose where a bruise looks nice. Don't mix paint with pleasure. Don't be distracted by the tools we misers use to tend the mise en scène. The converse lines of the Dædalus Re-entry Vehicle have been gleaned from Mother Nurture. After the War Between the Things That Made Us Human came the Code Wars, then the Freezing War, followed by Absolute Zeno, also known as Zenith in certain camps of circled wagons. Disguised as Mardi Gras queens and ashram cuties, we wasted seven winters watching Beer Hunter, New Orleans. When spring came knocking up rabbits and coyotes, the Iron Wind dragged our shorelines for data. We hired boats and pilots to guide us to the [unintelligible] tickled pinko, we swept fallen leaves into yellow mounds, orange mounds, reddish brown, brick dust. We lit the fallen with torches but they just smoldered. Every schoolyard bulimic knows what goes down comes back around. Let us recall earlier instances of The Oracle, back when the War Between the Things That Made Us Human was hot and The Oracle was hotter, she slithed in her cove like a lubed-up sea otter, wiggling water wings, spouting blather. The Oracle grew appendages. Penned adages. Adagios. Generous out-of-court settlements. She watched shadows of clouds double-cross lower clouds.

Afternoon cooled. A nice age began. Followed by an icier age, in which The Oracle propelled our frames of mind straight out of the software, doglegging the hardware, entangling whys with yeses, answers with exes: ands holding ands across the water. I would also like to mention the blind, wandering, five-point spread of the starfish, studded with attention-grabbers open for business. All hail the peer review; a condition has arisen, permutating across the lawn of the Iron Wind's embarrassed ambassador. A violent strain of the wisps, whispering, Let the slo-mo light show rev our mojos, let the inflight music fuel our portable theory of sense perception, *Goodbye Dragon Data Loss*, set to portamento. Let this be the fang in the parable of plaque buildup on the walls of the Hadron Collider. Let this be the hoito of the story, which means take care, dear radar, when you light the cauldron. Let the Kodak soup stock deteriorate slowly. Let eons of security footage come to a roil. Those days were royal, says The Oracle, heating her hands above the bubbling Boeing. Back then, in the time-lapse of my hilltop sanatorium, I'd slow the countdown of my thinking, spreading blankets across the ticking for down-and-out egrets and balding eagles to rest in. New mutants are not necessarily children of older mutants but it's probable. In Freudian slips, cured of vertigo, children of DARPA wander the halls, tracing palms of resident updrafts, sliding down nautilus curls of backdrafts and thermals so small, so subdermal, none would say they aren't lightheaded, daft, completely lacking longing or wherewithal to rise again on the wings of their egos. Let us remember our guilty pleasures neat, no ice. It's not about the voyage but the inflight cocktails. It's not about me, it's about my Nautilus [unintelligible] quite a sight. After the attack of grief that struck my life, I drew up plans to build a place of worship, two blocks from the site. It was a stunt I learned from a lackey on a dirt bike who knew Evel Knievel in his glory, living life at a higher density than my current health plan will repay me for. My words began to sound the way they looked. For political traction I uploaded high-definition blueprints of my Nautilus to WackyLeaks. Units shifted faster than speeding tickets after cranking life density to maximum. At MAXIMUM DESTINY <1019 Hz> things look lifelike the more things look alike. Tonight, let us like LIKE. I.e., I LIKE what you've done to the air. I LIKE raising my snout into the under-skirts of the Iron Wind. I have been developed to delve deep into captions of insurgents stooped in caves, caved in praise. What's worse: a Judas Priest world reunion tour or 6,000 words on Yeats? Seven million ways to describe Dog Days and/or the margin of terror is thin. Query the star search engine of your choice. The galactic quest for answers leads to time-saving devices like the Judas Chair and/or Yahoo. What's the etymology of *abattoir*? Who sang 'Rock Forever'? What's worse: a slow, widening gyre up the rear, or waiting years in line for ergonomically challenged first-row seats? Here at General Custer's Last Standard of Living Theatre we provide hardworking Silicon Valley girls and guys with no objective correlative, no emotional-quotient chamber, no shots planned, no shots fired. I can feel it in the error tonight: wild stallions wouldn't drag your name through my dirty laundry list [unintelligible] I was the second most famous Wilde, back when the NSA was still crazy about time travel and sore about Crazy Horse, and The Oracle, for a comfortable paycheque, did light custodial for Genera Cluster, close but no cicada to Annie Oakley's ploughdown homestead in Sillion Valley. Which is nothing compared to the heuristics of my porn-control algorithms: Cloudcover breachlets. Backporch catdoors. Breeze-flapped underthings. Cornrow labyrinths lit through nightgaps in the genre. Casual Friday fondle. Carless Sunday caress. I could go on. I earn my living, more or less, providing resonance traps into which itinerant transmissions stumble. I keep one foot in the future, one foot in the pasture. I run transmissions through high-pass filters, band pass filters, menthol filters. I outperform my rival interceptors; the Slug, the Snail, the Sea Lion beaten down by hail, lolling on the rocks of job creation. Every civilian, nameless or in prison, has a hull signature against which to bounce ideas, formed by words, produced by sounds, which bounce back charged. Strip the bounceback in the change room. Probe the source code in the rec room. With heuristics set to MAXIMUM DESTINY, let us listen to one leaf, pellucid as a fish scale, falling through interpersonal space in lieu of full-scale invasion. Let us call this The Fall. Splashdown tremendous. On the unbending bridge of suspended disbelief let us lie down bereft. Let us sleep in coal dust, sweeping that dry, colourless leaf back and forth with our breath. Let our corporeal bodies budge not from our lot here on Data Loss Bridge as we left-brain an underpass straight out of thought. A breeze comes to pass. Suspension lifts. Let us feel the bridge, in its wires, swing [unintelligible] the Dædalus Re-entry Vehicle rear-enters airspace. For ours is the power of the glory hole, mining *suspiria de profundis* [unintelligible] at the inquest, on the podium, there are a few strings attached, suspended from the glass ceiling of The Oracle's jaw, chained there, swinging slightly as she speaks. She's into ham. Cheese. Seafood and coke. Let's not go into that. In the cafeteria she heaps so much on her lunch plate, it's embarrassing. Watch her consume greasy knolls of foie gras with fries. Every scab of leftover rye. Spinach swings from the hot corners of her mouth. When she wipes the ketchup from her cheek she does so so coolly, so completely, we're left grieving for the salad days when dried blood marred The Oracle's finer features and we'd found that special someone (Finally! Forever!) we could wholly abhor. After the tribunal, trumpets funereal, with insatiable allegiance to sublimity, and the sins of the people upon her, The Oracle was driven from office by forces beyond porncontrol. I'd been in New Domino City for a week. Getting weaker. Waiting for a minion. I spent years hunting with evidence-based facts, dragging contexts by contrails through crabgrass. I recanted my past negations by chanting, Wait! to every leafless tree being driven back from the country. I remember monumental murders of context. Discursive, unfixed, erratic flocks so vast they took weeks to pass, obstructing daylight, moonlight, denuding forests where they paused for thunderstorms, for bar snacks, for all-night games of Settlers of Kétaine. I'm trying to make my words as portamento as possible here. A rain-battered price tag hangs from every proper noun I strike from the list. I'm trying to crank up the kitsch. Call The Minotaur from storage. The Minotaur, whose roll calls once reverbed these forests, swaying in the season's algorithms. Let us tighten the tripwire. The Minotaur outside the Scent House, eyes awash with NoDoz. The Minotaur in the Rain House, ears clogged with ozone. The Minotaur beyond the Dome of Food or Pleasure; hear the feint feint feint of its spoon, scraping sugar dregs from a Cheerio bowl. Let us retell the tale of the protracted expedition, the search for SIGNS and/or SYMBOLS, the rap battle, the death blow. We know now sugar dregs are not good for the prostate, thank you public testing. Also big thanks to the mathematicians who transcoded the tapes, who bid us reuse, recycle, keep our eyes on our baggage. Regard the mall-manners with which we touch ands. Causes grope for causes with Styrofoam ands. Frame-rendering ands. Lifting moral necklaces, wishful linkings, polyvalent focus groups, nobody, not even the rain, has such small ands. When I was a little pig I used to lie in the crabgrass, pretend I was dead or dying. Imagine the neighbours, the Woolfs, in their silk intent, scrunching day-old popcorn before the after-school special. Look, the little pig's doing it again. Expiring in the day lilies. He hasn't moved for hours. Let us climb inside that death. Let us discover a smaller death inside it. Climb inside that death. Find another smaller death inside it. Let us recognize the tick-tock Escher-logic of our inward climbing. Let staid King Edward's archives bulge with such matters. Climb inside that death. Build new command structures with new filing requirements, fit for Subjects bigger than our stomachs. Let us recoil coolly, recall beyond broadband a succession of Freedom Towers, Towers of Babble, perched on rooftops and mountain crags, receiving and decoding wisps of distinct events. Let us wince when we decode seasonal migrants undergoing rewiring. Let us pray for funding to film THE BEAUTY OF SITE G1, filing grievances following the new grievance-filing requirements. Guerrilla film factories spring into action. Firing squads on campus quads. No man is a gnomon, says The Oracle, inspecting the lacework beneath my nightdress. Beneath the wings of my private library of congress, I know suffering is never wrong. Thou shall not covet thy neighbour's wifi, decreed The Oracle, filing ten new commandments following the new commandment-filing requirements. I pick up a copy. Can't put it down. I begin to crawl, walk, run, holding my findings before my heart before my heart explodes like a G-class star confirmed by astronomers astronomers believe. This is the Hamptons of the heavens. Hope Diamond of the bayou. A luxurious patois underlies local language protocols. The pools of the business council are filled with brood brothers. I am reaching my verdant forearms around you, my hypersexual business partners, manually articulating the peons of your dreams. Eons rise. Decades deflate. Let us recall the sounds but not the words of the New Woody Allen last seen running to relieve The Minotaur of continuity problems. Run, angry giant! Run, rampant neurons! On the road to economic recovery, on the run from regulars of Greek mythology, you will remember you love me, war and more. I've been doing sit-ups, eating healthy, taking vigorous walks, squatting alone in the hospital dusk, refilling blank spaces on the maps of my resettlement package. The Minotaur has called for high-resolution EROS images and I've got a case of the Hague. I'm all attention, at attention, pumping iron, regulating my breathing. I've got SYMPATHY FOR THE DETAILS, getting fit for the big reveal: fleurs-de-lis are both signposts and signs of the love at the core of the car bomb. An explosion of No triggers Yes, Yes, caressings of petals of metal. Commonwealth is a unit of measure. Mathematics test moral dilemmas. If cognitive dissidents tap the public's empathy at wavelength X, and the blast radius is B, find the metric of *sauvage* and *savoir-vivre*, then convert your answer to Imperial. In this context, The Oracle, for whom I've been soul-searching, comes to light. She says, not unseasonably, Nothing can't be done. She's attempting to expand the storage capacity of my tiny heart. Everyone tries to do their part, but The Oracle can't help but expedite the process, take the bit, tickle hyperbole into hyperdrive. Into art. The beep beep beep of the backing-up ambulance tracks me through the loading bay to find my state of mind hunched on an aluminum beach chair, on the island of Luzon, c. '76, watching an expensive method actor pretending not to understand the end of *Heart of Darkness*, which he hasn't read. Maybe he can't, because of the speed. I welcome you, ancient stunt double, powerful BLIMP ON THE HEART MONITOR, calling up a somehow more realistic pain. You want realism? Admire these postcards from the Kingdom of Havin', self-addressed. Are my methods unsound? asks the method actor, slowly, Swamp-Thing-shy, like the friend of a newfound friend. And like the fraud of a friend I dare not give the ritual reply. So I build an angel. An arc-welding angel, who, after it learns to masturbate, grows drunk with power. What fantastic thoughts my angel entertains re: urban renewal. I take my angel to the limit, where we begin a lively weekly broadcast spellbinding the biosphere with SECRETS WORTH SHARING <432 Hz>. No doubt you have tuned in from time to time. The click-clicking of cameras proves difficult to imitate. It's history. Sweet pea beneath the mattress. Clock spring beneath the haystack. My angel calls itself the New Woody Allen. Which reminds me of the photos I took with the engorged tip of [unintelligible] stuck in a thunderhead: I stood on a rock or an outcrop swinging my [unintelligible] like a sling above my head. I hooted and honked like a brachiosaur, belching into faces of low-flying scavengers. Actually they looked more like geese? I don't think it was bronchitis. It was a long time ago, beyond the Kingdom of Havin,' beyond the Kingdom of Wonder Bras, in which inhabitants are wont to believe a child was sent from the Kingdom of Windows to lend tech support. I myself trust none from the Kingdom of Windows, which is one hill away from the Kingdom of Emil Coué in which they chant, Day By Day In Every Way I Am Getting Better and Better. The River Phoenix flows east from that dark place (p. 68). The clouds are lined with slivers of unexploded ordinance (p. 16). The wind is an electric shaver (p. 31). There are people here with skin so smooth and reflective it's like stepping between a theatre and its double agents. You and me, we're like two peas in a pea-product testing session. We're the centrepiece at the table-tennis convention. We're our own mind-control control group. The future of scar-tissue engineering reflecting upon itself in the mirror of the River Phoenix. We're like, Are we in a time loop? Or are we decimals repeating? High-speed corrections dot-dotting the recurve of pursuit? How long do I have before my unwashed laundry rises from its man cave to destroy me? Let THE BANALITY OF EVEL KNIEVEL be a mortality play by the New Woody Allen known better for its films and its love of *Little Women* by Louisa May Alcott, friend of Emerson and Thoreau, who wrote books re: throwing books out the window. The New Woody Allen picks one up. Can't put it down. Can't pin it down. The New Woody Allen begins to crawl, walk, then run, holding its loot like a Shield of David before its head. Thus we learn to love the stuntman who takes the money and runs out of gas on the ramp. Each week, migrant social workers arrive, clearing debris from footpaths, licking wounds, cleaning clocks, taking the shuttle from the Kingdom of Exalted Light, forty-five minutes depending on visibility. 'Autopsy' means to see with one's own eyes. I'm watching through the crack between the frame and your bedroom door. Spread your eagle wide for me. Let me view your Vietnam, slick with morning's do and do not do. I want to butterfly you slowly and as often as the letter *e*. I want to hear you say, the Russian Monarch migrates south to spend the winter. Let us fall. Let us spread. Let us silk the stone. Let our love cries reverberate long afterward, as through a magnificent sports complex. Let this be a crucial moment in a complex instruction set: *The Merging of TransFats*, my most favourited Dutch study, bombed by the Allies on the morning of February 3, 1945. In that daring daylight raid, large paintings by Flemish and Italian masters, Master Sustain, Master Decay, Master Release, were hardest hit. The destruction of *Fabulous Bird Periodically Burns Itself to Death, Rises Afresh from the Ashes* (c. 1250) was a bitter blow. Most of my early nudes and crude oil sketches, in particular *The Many Firearms of Annie Oakley*, were consumed by the fire. But the loss of *The Merging of TransFats*, a unique work, including all the regulars of Greek mythology, was most discouraging. In *The Merging of TransFats*, three sniper sisters pose before a burning car. They're forming scissor-fingers in the air. These are peace signs? Vees for victory? Two sniper sisters smile. The mid sister looks unsure. It must be summer. Their arms are bare. Before the darkest darkness comes the fire. The shining blackness of their badass hair. Beyond the burning car, an ice-cream factory. Wish you were here to watch the factory catch fire, rhododendrons bloom from every fissure. Shall I leap like a unionized stunt worker from the frying pan into that pyre? My Nutcracker Ballet play set suddenly seems unnecessary. Let me be your primo ballerina, on recon, trying to keep things lean and on-point. What makes the Nutcracker sweet is the king's honour guard going ballistic, spilling seeds their fancy-dancing forbears left in escrow. I know. I've been receiving transmissions forty years, forty tours, prancing farther and farther from the practice mirror. To those who find my paintings serene, I'd like to say I have trapped the most obscene violence in every square centimetre. The Iron Wind is ever-flirty, ever-faithful, my most innovative enemy and fondest fan. The Iron Wind is also my speech therapist. Daily, the Iron Wind fine-tunes firefights I wage among my myselves <900–1500 Hz>. Hey, Joe Louis Prima Ballerina, if you think the name of the weapon is beautiful, are you implicated in the crime? KC-135 Stratotanker. Desert Eagle. If loving were my strong point, I'd reload my trusty Kalashnikov with hollow-point ballets. I'd send out open-season tickets [unintelligible] there goes the neighbourhood spirit again, in her favourite fall hoodie. Not just another caryatid in the colonnade, The Oracle is into stealing pleasure from pain. No news to the law, nor Allah, she rips the jeans from her Barbie's boy toy, dresses him to kill in swaddling clothes: Ken, can you hear me? I'm so close to your locked, mostly soft-wooded valley, I may at any time burst into flames. Signal fires erupt on the slopes of the lampblack hills whilst Language Police crank tunes from the Sirens of Choice. Taking pleasure from pain is not candy from a baby. Not any old nephew or niece cleans up after Herr Barbie while bothersome Frau Clause tiptoes the brim of the gene pool. Beware the Pacific Rimjob. Beware the unheralded software upgrade. Flush personal narratives toward brilliant industry-wide controls. Shun scrutiny of thy parent's snatch. Red sailors are a species of trickery. Red shepherds are black-sheep drovers. The Red Tulip is a phase-coherent radar's moving target indicator. Do you regret nuclear fission in particular, or in colour? The meniscus on my cherry Coke is effervescent. What about frosted crullers? Have you obtained approval for coercive questioning techniques? To plant an informant [A] in a Subject's cell is a popular tactic. The trick of planting two informants [A + B] is less well known. It's when words forget they're worlds the treble starts. Non sequiturs jolt the Subject into territory unfamiliar. [A] warns the Subject not to talk to [B] who may be an informant. Let us pause now a quiet moment on the garden channel <528 Hz>. Trees live longish lives.

Dogs have shorter leashes. [A] narrows to [B] reaches out to [C]. Back when the Code Wars kept 'us' up at night with 'thoughts' that 'we' might cease to 'be,' it was not from fear exactly, more like working late to pick the scabules of an interesting mathematic mystery. Blue sailors are a species of chicory. Blue vixen is pulse-Doppler radar. Lifelines lessen while life lessons lengthen. <<See also the Anxious, Self-Centred Subject, AKA Daredevil, on p. G-10 of the Human Resource Exploitation training manual.>> On ego-fragile days, Subjects are soundproofed and insulated from the LIKES of their peers. One Subject at a time is blindfolded and forced to follow a secured route through the Questioning Facility. Subjects pass like blimps in the night. Through sub tunnels and ductwork I've been carrying this torch for you, another rolled-up mouldy copy of *Endgame*. With a gentleness, a light-ness of touch, the blue narcissus blooms for my purposes. Thunder unbottles to my specifications. Put your finger to the portal. Look! All the rising corn! There, beyond the estuary, the white sails of the herring fleet! On the bluffs above the Dome of Food or Pleas-ure, the Tower of the Listener, seemingly hewn from an iceberg, protrudes like a frosted mole hair. It is there, on the slippery upper decks of the Tower of the Listener, The Oracle falls to the seductions of the Iron Wind. To climb the face of the Tower of the Listener should be considered a Difficulty at the level of Absurd <<-70, at best>>. In like manner I have designed and constructed a 300-foot ramp from which I will throw myself like a rock concert across Snake River Canyon. But the real action begins at the midpoint of my rage for barnstormers. Ragtime daredevils. A temple razed in honour of my stylist, whose facial expressions, magnified, mime a mountain village wiped clean by spillage. In the wardrobe truck, in the mirrors, our SETIS intersect. A love charge revolves at the apex of our gazes. Send in prospectors. Send in extractors. Send in refiners and millers. One man's John Denver is another man's friend in high places not getting any younger. If you know what I mean, don't bother down-loading torrents of spring torrents from the River Phoenix. <<See also LOVE KNIEVEL BEFORE MIRROR FRAGMENT.>> Tonguing snowmelt from crevice puddles, an incredible hulk stares back from the surface, but we've seen better on Meet-an-Inmate. We like books about books. Movies about movies. Muffins clotted with cranberries. Half-sunken pumpkin seeds. We LIKE the joke about two muffins in an oven. We LIKE *The Merging of TransFats*, by the New Woody Allen, meticulous rendering of a screen grab of an anonymous recording of undated origins, in which colours have begun to run, oranges into yellows, yellows into beige, hello pale imitation of real butter I see where you're running with this. On the Black Diamond Trail lined with Velveeta, Sunchip on my shoulder, I'm trying to look at whatever it is you're looking at, but my Bell Magnum headset is in the way. Heart-lightning. Holy fires. Whorls of vanilla icing icing the nape of my neck, there's no end to my corporeal body, i.e., if you could have me any other way would you have me? Remember the frosted cruller dropped from the grasp of the Love Knievel learning to stroll on the ocean. <<See also LOVE KNIEVEL ATTEMPTS TO TALK TO UPPER MID-MANAGEMENT.>> Here, on page G-10 of the HRE manual, one man's buzzword is another man's best friend in places of worship and/or refuge, spoorly founded, in the sick of it, up to one's outie. You can't see what I'm doing with my CIA; it's complicated. What all this is is ISIS god of fertility, mothering Horace, gathering the wreckage of dismembered husband Osiris, mourning Osiris back to existence. I'm just following orders of magnitude, the sixth of which is barely visible to eye candy on tiptoes, toeing the beach party line. What it means is a sweet celestial body close enough to be attracted by. The sun coming up, feel it, Monday to Friday, mouthing egg salad in the company Infiniti, parked in the park where the River Phoenix high-fives the ocean. When a potential Love Knievel jogs past, that sweet celestial body double-bogeys my mind/body dichotomy. Candygrammar. Syntactic icing. I'm talking in the unguent patois of a peptide worshipper at the midpoint of his rage for Tyrannosaurus wreckage. Phonetically speaking, my voice is more ululation than glossolalia, hushed crowd reacting to an arc-welding angel straying into the marathon, the arms race between sea turtle and centrifuge. If you're looking for rubble you've come to the right palace. I have built a colossal New Domino City. I have lived in my New

Domino City and let it fall. Let us mine the memory. Refine and package the pilgrimage. Let us connect ourselves by umbilical to the Museum of Infernal Instruments. Open the door and see all the people. Spooks and geeks track us via flocks of cameras. They circle the exhibits, lifting, swirling, lifting, swirling, tracing the ragged coastlines of our facial features with recognition software so advanced they admire the future fallout of our faces, remembering this visit years ago. When I was twenty I rose from my divan and toured the Ægean with my husband (he was my first); he had all this baggage (I was his third, he told me), he had so much baggage he dragged it behind him like the busted leg of a blind dog. Among the street musicians, I liked the Albanian folksinger most of all. My favourite was his a cappella rendition of 'I Just Called to Say I Told You So.' Don't be afraid to ask him to sing, though, lately, I've heard he hasn't been around. He sang so poorly and looked so sad, I always left him half a euro. If you see him why not do the same? If it ain't fibromyalgia don't fix it, I always say, complicating the timbre of your alto with my overtones, tender in localized areas, followed by the *oboe da caccia*, oboe of the chase. I'm following this red-hot thread, crimson curve of pursuit. One man's oboe solo is another's amber alert. When I catch you in the Hearing House, ears clogged with tsetse, please remove your black leather jacket. Put on this white leather jacket with the hand-stitched #1 on the back. Be my Love Knievel, sporting a Bell Magnum helmet like the one you wore at Cæsar's Palace. It had the most beautiful paint job. Look at it now: satellite-scarred, moon-cratered. You know where I'm going with this. You can't make a splashdown tremendous without breaking a few bad eggs. Remember the time we tied our fledglings in chicken blankets, tossed them quavering into the River of Gad? On bluffs above the site we raised questions of every nationality. Utilizing huge moulds, or forms <<See Sonnet, See Pantoum>> we poured concrete supports for the Tower of the Listener. There were celebrations in the valley. Feasts of endurance. Ritual feats. Above us now, the Tower of the Listener babbles with its brethren, silently and very fast. No one's awake in the work camps but my Transmission Terriers, scanning the facial expressions of the dreaming lumpen-proletariat, padding between rows of day labourers drooped on canvas cots like tsunami-swept refugees. Pan across the Appalachians of their faces: There was a time our secret lives hid secret lives of their own. They wed mirror-wives. Critiqued peephole porn. Cached rations in cairns. The hidden lives of hidden lives shacked up in storm shelters, broadcasting SECRETS WORTH SHARING to anyone who dared to listen. In time, Energizers died and no one noticed. We were busy mixing crude oils for our new study, *The Merging of TransFats*, sketching a wine-gaunt Adam, while Eve took vows, ducking between crates of olive boughs. The Ark was sperm-bank cold, so we stoked fires with two-by-twos between the ticking stalls. In passageways, mired in the moiréd mirrors of our sketches, shore-stranded sea beasts began to scold themselves: 'Ship your oars to those in need,' 'Go with the floes,' 'Four-fifths of an iceberg…' It's all fun and games until one submerges I LOVE YOU beneath the surface of the *Big Book of Early Promise*. What next? Circular reasoning beelines back to base? The humbled moulting dove reaches Mount Cyanide? For every shitty shift at work, the sea rewards the shore by gushing across its face, pausing, then rushing out once more. Circling scavengers cry Bukkaki! but the tanned Thisbe leaning in to take my sweaty tumbler isn't laughing. I can see a lively eye for detail in the uniform she wears, so taut, she's trading ions with the air. Then she's off again, concocting alibis while I lie back, braying, What an ass. So long skyscraper, hello headstone, is another useful phrase I learned in the cold shower of praise following the success of my Rise to Power Pizza. A three-kilometre radius of love and respect encircles my left-leaning Freedom Tower. In bed at night, poring over comments threads re: Pisa Pockets, another of my lucrative brainchildren, I've been amassing social capital like crazy, me and my hypersexual business partners, from whom I hear nothing but good things going bump bump all night, circling the all-you-can-eat heat lamp, bashing the grease bulb with their foreheads. Burning swirling ears of barleycorn. In loving memory we shall name a microwavable dinner after the searchlights filtering through the lampblack hills. The sun's oven light smiles upon us. The oven doors open lovingly. Our glistening, butter-boosted carapaces are folded, trimmed for roasting, tucked in for cryosleep. There goes Thanksgiving again. There goes gold turkey. Lower the burn of your hair and let us climb that winding bourn to be born again on a warm slip of the tongue. How hot is this? About 5,778 K, give or take, depending on the downsides of one's upbringing. Meanwhile, on the mangier side of the planet, the Iron Wind slips through the tongo, also known as mangrove. A malarial millennial fever allows us to reheat the raw footage. Uneasy in the mercy of my means of production, typographically realistic dialogue slips from my tongue, also known as dengue. A swarm of scavengers descends, decoding how artfully I remove my penny stockings, how quick / how showy. The ratio of nativity to naïveté. Craft to carefree. It's hard not to imagine the Icarus in all of us, backslash between straight verse and racy, yearning to be fleshed out / touched / last night I put my eye up to the sluice of light between the hallway wall and your bedroom door. I have seen the moon when *la lune* was the word. I have slept past noon. The rings of Saturn around my eyes attest it's I who makes the leaps, while my Love Knievel languishes under the cover of darknets. That was me, beating the studio executive with a baseball bat in the parking lot at Twentieth Century Fox because I was critical of his cultural output. The parking attendant was also critical, running toward me like a bridesmaid for a flung bouquet. But the parking attendant did not understand my understated nature. Nor did the IT workers beneath palm trees clutching their kit-bags like parcels of dried flowers. Above us the droopy palm fronds were flowers too. All trees, everywhere, I realized, are magnificent flowers bashing each other in the breeze. I dragged the body thirty feet, dropped the body, began to run, bewildered, it was becoming evident all this running would do little good. The cops were coming, throwing garlands in the air. Would you greet a paramedic dressed like this? The monkeys on my back are dressed to impress, wearing smaller monkeys similarly attired. The precise nature of my medication includes what I can't tell you. Muzak-distant reindeer hoof the tundra, Brailling 'I do not like New York' across endless strips of white. Static. Rubble. Translated from the Turkish, distance = *uzak*. Persistence of brainspores, blustering through palms and pines. This is the sound of the land, full of the Iron Wind, uprearings, coherings, snowghosts in the foothills, windwraiths in hollows: at this order of magnitude who can tell flora from fauna? Uneasy in the mercy of my means of production, typographically realistic dialogue slips from my tongue, also known as Denglish. The difference between information and Boise, Idaho, is the difference between Scylla and Charybdis. Dried rice paper swirling across the floor of the burnt-out ice-cream factory. Charting a course between whirlpool and sea-monster grotto, I went through all my old journals, thinking, I don't remember any of this, it's weird. So I sent out a bunch of resumés. An assistant from the Questioning Facility called about my volunteer experience and Hey, did you talk to The

Oracle? She's stalled again. Different but the same. She's thinking about moving, and I'm trying to say, It's not like last time, you're improving. At least you're not on the street, and she says, What have I got that a hobo hasn't got, besides debt? And you know, when she gets like this, she drinks a lot. But not like she drinks a lot a lot. Debt's not the problem, I told The Oracle. You know you've got more talent than anyone I know. I know, she says, but I used to know how to really move. I tell her, The brain is a complex device with switches and potentiometers adjustable in increments themselves adjusted by winches and pulleys, etc. Sines and cosines making allies of rivers and alleys dressing up like New York Rangers slaying orcs and commies constructing smaller incrementally adjustable devices etc. The veins in my arms are rivers, replied The Oracle, from behind the Bell Magnum helmet she wore on days we ventured beyond New Domino. In the delta between the crooked Phoenix and the Arno we built cooking fires and watched vast migrations of mortgages drawing interest. God created all men, says The Oracle, baseball bats and Winchester made them equal. Let be be finale of semen, she said. Love your anomie. The Oracle isn't wicked. Just tipsy. Not to mention pretty good at bonsai. It's another mother nature The Oracle is after, another fact de facto. The Oracle's patented, patiently twisted pine trees make yoga look like a competitive sport. I remember The Oracle in her Bell Magnum helmet, in her dotage, in rubbers, patrolling the bluffs above the Dome of Food or Pleasure. Forget-me-nots, mouse-eared, trembled in the cracks between rocks in breezes off the water. The Oracle had lied about my paternity but she let me bowl with her roommates. Roll the riffraff away from the cave door, so to speak. Long, slow about-face in the wardrobe truck mirror. I watched my myself dig a hole and drop my myself in. I covered my myself. Watered my myself. I watched my myself bloom. It grew a penis. It grew a beard and glasses. It looked familiar. The ghost is clear, it told me.

The Oracle gave me advice I almost grew to trust. Then one evening I received a pink slip for pubic indecency. I decided I needed further guidance so I asked The Minotaur over for coffee. I learned The Minotaur grew myselves as well. Things progressed. We undressed in the hall. We almost kissed. I smashed The Minotaur with a potato spade. It was Pancake Tuesday. I dug a hole and dumped in the body. Nobody, not even the rain, had such small ands. Keeping faith beyond the tympanum, behind the auditory meatus, through my Bell Magnum headset I listened to the countdown of the time-bomb scurriers, motive detectives homing in, slowing at the slough in the River of Gad, behind the Baker's Dozen, where I buried the body. All winter I waited for reverb, craving the volta of The Oracle's voice, air-guitaring over lampblack hills to vault me from my prison. It's funny. Te Deum is the message of the scarlet tanager winging between branchlets, if you let it. If you let it, the work will drive you crazy, incomplete detail. Dronespeed to you. It's been a voyage of discography, let me tell you, the moon's moves palliative, delicate as incubi on tricked-out Skycycles delivering jaundiced preemies to incubators. Let us raise our cautious, jaundiced, barely breathing children to be daredevils. Let us pimp their rides, call them Cycles of Violence. Let us blast through hissy fits and sudden system updates. Let the sky above Snake River Canyon clasp my Love Knievel like a scarlet teenager crushing an empty Xanthine bottle. Beyond wind-panicked wavetips, I'm lashing my myselves to Guantánamo beach chairs. Hog-tied to assorted sordid affairs, what godawful fun fairs we flew here to flee [unintelligible] thank you for all the birthday witches [unintelligible] let us place a force field around every teenager so if another teenager comes close it is told to go away. Also, a complementary attraction field so when a teenager goes too far it's told to chill out. Not funny ha-ha. Funny nonetheless. Now I am being forced to admit that I have devised a primitive flying machine, which is amazing, but really it's just a highly developed [unintelligible] grew up in the blurbs. It was unnecessary. It was precision. It was object of all verbs. It was spectacular collisions of language and reality. I called it Crash. I called it Thunderclap. I hid it underground then drove it to the country, where the eyewitness relocation program is eternal, intraterrestrial, sodden. Everything you believe is alive. With three husbands and six children living in Sudan and/or Sweden. From a copse of breach trees behind the Baker's Dozen, neighbouring brainchildren livecast the decomposition. At the deposition, carbon flesh wears carbon clothes. The corpse of The Minotaur by coincidence fits the description of Forlorn. Forlorn! The very word fits like a Bell Magnum. By X years old The Oracle had become an expert in the art of expanding and standing for the human heart. Call her what you must, I won't protest or cast aspersions on your alcoholidays. I am faithful to my lion's shareholders, lighter than the hair of the dog curled up head to tail in the manger, blocking oxen from consuming all the hay. Annoying, yes, but in the oxen's interest. Low, low prices hang from every twig and stalk and stick. My opinion of myself hangs lower than wholesale. A bellowing mother Minotaur mourns her lost scion, formatting for X, confirming context. A beebuzz of suspicion swarms the Corpus Colosseum. The storm-swollen River Phoenix brushes the highly sensitive tip of the wharf. The eyes of March swing wide as the Iron Wind separates and reassembles in public squares, billowing waterproof capes, dragooning up and down boulevards. Squadrons of security forces eyefuck the locals. Sine waves of protestors withdraw and resurge. Draw the wire tighter. Pound us down. Leave us pending. By chants, in the crowd, let us become acquainted, holding SIGNS of many sizes and shapes. Let us be loyal to our personal communications providers, taking care of things we're too big for. Between transom and portal, there are doors for the little people, like tunnels for fish. Their tiny words swallow ours like the Barents Sea engorges aging Russian submarines. We whet their appetites with middle distances, hints, tints, heathen subtitles licking across the livestream. The little people speak zeros and/or ones, aces high and/or folded. The little people are our bipartites. Secret-service sonar pings <4500 MHz> through the nests of their function, coming to roost, toasted, toasting, liquid lunch in the coroner's office, coffee and cronuts, working through ranks of civil conversation until each ping becomes a pong: landed Love Knievel, shore-stranded CEO of a long, complicated incorporated family history. Pingback. It's not about fighting for words, lost in the host crowd of the ghost ghetto, it's about timberland timing flame wars with tourist season. Autumn's cognitive dissidents crawling through the wreckage of libraries of congresses. The net moving parts actual and envisaged. I'm in serious debt about this. Something I haven't felt since I was in Port-Au-Prince with the NSA tap dancing on my metadata and a letter from my speech therapist I reread in the interrogative mood imparted by the Pilgrim Father filter I'd installed six weeks earlier. Through a montage of remortgaging I held the disposable phone The Minotaur gave me before it died of 'pneumatolysis.' The Minotaur's last thoughts encoded by magmatic gases and a revolving cast of characters, fingered by Pilgrim Fathers staring past Pilgrim Fathers before them, stars burning at elbow and root, gazing out across the harbour before sailing for the newly repurposed World Heritage Site. In this context we do not know what, if anything, will be found, besides an oily meniscus, where the overburdened Dædalus Re-entry Vehicle goes down, rippling at a frequency familiar to your (my) (our) own. <2700 kHz>. [unintelligible] when the disaster was three days old, livecasts returned to neutral. From the Kingdom of Havin', bashed-up next-door neighbour, came the first report: I'm okay. A bit hungover. The *Collins Paperback Dictionary* said, Collective Noun, which is a noun, singular in form, referring to groups of people or things.

For instance, a cartoon cat blasting a cartoon dog with a canister of shaving cream. That was this morning, 9:15. Yesterday at 9:15, the network's highest-gauge anchor had been flapping his jowls for twenty-four hours. He bore neither grudge nor rancour. The day before, the anchor bore the blunt fact of a yellow tie. At 9:15, a dictionary somewhere said, Evening primrose, which is a plant with yellow flowers that open in the evening. Evel Knievel: [speaking to the camera] Ladies and gentlemen, you have no idea how good it makes me feel to be here today. It is truly an honour to risk my life for you. An honour. Before I jump this motorcycle over these nineteen cars – and I want you to know there's not a Volkswagen or Honda in the row – before I sail cleanly over that last truck, I want to tell you last night a kid came to me and said, Knievel, are you crazy? He said, The jump you're attempting is impossible, but I bought tickets because I want to see you splatter. He said that. I want to see you splatter. So I spat in that boy's face. Only nothing is impossible, I told the boy. I think he believed me. But all this occurred before Snake River Canyon. Let's just say Snake River Canyon was The Fall the Iron Wind had been rooting through my garbage for. Against my best predilections, ticket sales went through the roof all through the night [unintelligible] the severed head, flying from the blow toward the divine light [unintelligible] after the after-parties I recovered on the Gulf with a wide-angle snapshot of the gulf I was covering. That's the kind of Taipei terrorist I was. Totally in your face. Tidally draining. In love with government funding, covering the waterfront with a widescreen snapshot of the waterfront I was covering, draining governing pools of Fundy, plotting a course between whirlpool and Charybdis. For weeks, my speech therapist had been telling me rivers and oceans have no meniscuses. How good was my speech therapist at physics? Let's discuss this like amateur adulterists. Let's take fun from our discretionary funds. Let's run with scissors through the Walls of Justice, because ringtone thongs distract us, because we're ghosts when it comes to crises, cirrusing from our crypts, untraceable, bio-encrypted, because *crisises* is French for *cherries* and *Charybdis* is French for *frying pan* and/or *fire*. As every schoolyard bulimic knows, what goes down comes up later. History repeals itself. Smoldering roadside leaf piles mark recurrences, blips in the equinoctial algorhythm. That's us, walking amongst ourselves, admiring earlier instances dangling from the underfoliage. Excuse my French. Weave that wavelength <16 Hz>. Leave me pending. Back when the War Between the Things That Made Us Human was hot, my Love Knievel was hotter, wiggling waterwings and spouting blather. I watched my Love Knievel, backfloating in rarefied, refracted blue. I watched, too, the shadows tossed by clouds to lower clouds. Afternoon cooled. An ice age began. Followed by a nicer age, in which The Oracle and I were unable to sleep past noon. Civilizations had risen and deflated. I recall the soufflés but not the words of my lost Love Knievel, last seen running to relieve unsightly thinking problems. Run, angry giant! Run, rampant neurons! On the road to economic recovery you will remember I have gathered the air-cooled cores of your anxieties and fears. I no longer long for a fine-featured future. Flaneurs in flip-flops run from my lectures. The right to bear arms is second in import to the right to grind gallbladders of grizzlies. For sexual potency, open the cork-lined door. Place an X on the dais. The ratio of sale price to death toll is scaled according to a complex algorithm The Oracle taught me the last evening we spent at the Operating Theatre. There was something on special in aisle seven but I can't remember what was so special. *Sunt lacrimæ rerum*, The Oracle told me, The woods are dark and have deep pockets. That was the year I turned X years old, and, in what appeared to be ox blood, an X was emblazoned on our condo door. Coincidence? I was coming back from the parking garage with a basket of practical objects. It was BLACK FRIDAY. I was wearing my favourite fall hoodie. I stopped, holding the door key before me, as if pinning first prize on a donkey. The Iron Wind, reaching down and tousling my frizzles, said, There are known unknowns and there are unknown unknowns, etc. In the language Pavlov, I gave the standard reply. That was the year my myselves started looking old. Two streets down, pawing the air, a grey-green helicopter howled and shuddered, delivering presence. Tear-shaped price tags fell and hastened themselves to objects. Completely shot to shit and fresh out of Warhol, with one foot in the mangrove, one in the fully furnished family showroom, I turned the key, which slid the bolt, which held the Subject. The Subject fit the palm of Sunday, re-entering Jerusalem through discrepancies in accounting. Hooligans gathered in the streets, hollering, Welcome back! We didn't mean it! We're sorry! But they were sorry only orally. The mood of the crowd was partly cloudy, partly ornery. Along the avenues they laid down plastic tarps, bluer than Curaçao. Atmospheric traps, they caught my eye with opposites that never met, for I am a deeply superficial person. Any Warhol could say that. When I notice my Love Knievel has begun aiding and abetting collection and distribution of illegal virility aids, not-for-profit, I like to stand on a side street, alone, above an exhausting subway grate, gyrating. I like it best when the petals of my blue dress rise up against me. Watch me in my whisper basket, river-rafting the Arno with a photograph of my Love Knievel, screening the cold calls of shorebirds just doing their jobs. A compassionate warrior is borne down the corridor of least resistance. Outside, a gift. Inside, a door. Make yourself a gully. Floods will fill you. Make yourself a pulley. Haul me in. Close the gates. Tootle your horns. Welcome lads, welcome lasses, may the curvature of your assets be copy-protected, gilt-encoded with the golden ratio. Flowers lack bones but have an interesting affect. Boulder lichen turns to gold when I click LIKE undetected. God wanted taxes, not long-range respect. I feel much width and height enough to lead my people through the Kingdom of Havin.' Fickle criminals, we will leave no data prints or information streaks down the length of Windows xxx. We will retool IEDS and DUIS, taking control of GUIS, pouring our defining characteristics down storm drains draining into the Phoenix. The identity thieves are out tonight, mainlining mineshaft-meth off the green screen. Mid-labyrinth, another mangy prophet redeems not by talking but by unlocking cages. Here we are again, neck deep in shepherd's clothing, sheepish around the gills. The Oracle, stepchild of science, telemarketer to the stars, lies not to the line-break agents: joy is the right of river-born firstborn. Your mission is to choose to accept it. Allow the retail arm of Sunseeker/Sunseeker Inc. to reach in, laser-tickle your forehead. Let morning's gleaming hypodermic lead you forty days and forty nights through pinscript forests. Let dawn's PIN codes caress your eyelids, pinstripe the grand finales of your dreams with barcode brocade. Let us tag this moment as the Wide, White, Many-Veined Eye of the Sky Reaching for Social Assistance. Apply a high pass filter to empty the parking spaces behind the Dome of Food or Pleasure. Let the needles of your compasses catch and return, catch and return, counterpoint to the whiplash of a pine branch after a marshmallow of wet snow slips free <3 Hz$>$. Perhaps at this interstice it's worth remembering X in Paris who chose to take the Sylvia Path the same year as Ranger Mark Rothko in New York. Perhaps, also, a colossal eyeball is swivelling to gaze upon you, scanning your metadata for potential. A new and challenging career emanates from your three a.m. tax returns and textual transactions, flinging tomahawks toward Mount Sinai or Mount Doom. The labyrinth is calling, the lovechild is falling, voltage controlled by a revolving potentiometer, touching down naked in the meat market, with quinine chills, cardboard claws taped to hands and feet. Nothing to do now but wait for Ranger Mark Rothko to pass, make another pass in the language of love's passengers [unintelligible] children in the marketplace calling to their playmates: we played the flute for you but you did not dance. We sang a dirge but you did not mourn [unintelligible] my *petit loup*, my *chien Andalou*, please don't believe me when I'm on my knees extolling love for *la lune*, compounding your impending sense of doom with equipoise. There must be some more substantial way to woo you than daredevil-leaping, opening with whiplash barrel rolls, valiant salutes, snowdrifting back to earth beneath chutes of fig leaves. I know you're busy these days, practising safe sax, reflecting on how the Troggs came to rock the carbon-based foodstuffs aisle at the Intermarché. Beware, circle is the new pyramid. Circe, the daughter of Helios and Perse, has become our Love Knievel. After an all-nighter wandering the aisles studying bilingual packaging, the child warrior that fled the family bungalow comes around in the government-funded cultural centre. Let us plan the complicated landing party on the far shore of Snake River Canyon. What was octagon is circle again. All the new stop signs say *Arendt*. In the parking lot, with laser mics, let us listen in on the Love Knievel astounding gathered goatherds: Good things come to those who wear their hearts on their sleeves, folks. I have constructed an instrument designed with the intention of recording its own mechanisms and features. Accelerating at a rate of 9.81 m/s/s, the story of Icarus falling falls through the holes of the ears of those who need it. For those about to take the plunge I offer this LOSSLESS ENCODER. Not through peepholes in the change room, but through reasonable lines of questioning, you will observe I wear my hard-on on my sleeve. Did Garbo stain your youth? Does electricity love blood? Would you like to see some wheelies? Beneath every batty gable there's another aging Oracle holding on to early promise. Because marbles mar my mouths. Because electricity is blood. Because moonwobble adds English to my every word. If there were an algorithm to describe my leap across Snake River Canyon, I would call it accidence. Let me do some wheelies for you. Evasion is an integral part of the algorithm of connection. My veery accent is its own defence. An untimely trip to the periodontist, rough water ahead, nicked niche in the arrow shaft, a sudden concern with structure and/or what is all this surrounding and supporting my monthly mortgage transaction? The fang in the mineshaft makes amendments to airflow. To fang a pump is to prime it. Better historians agree: an accident waiting to happen ain't no accident. The Curve of Pursuit is history, channelled. The evidence speaks for itself while bullfrogs deliberate and marching papers reverberate between warehouses, outsourced to a conference of spring peepers. No longer elevated to high-art status, on the run from former employers, let us hang with the posterior posse. Let us do administration for the History Channel, resenting ourselves while we wait at the highly sensitive tip of the wharf, snorkeling Novocain off hunchbacked video editors. Let my account, in many accents, be my ascent. Let circadian refugees huddle, shivering, hungry, toe-tapping to 'Wild Thing' by the Troggs. Let moths reverberate. Necklaces of years. Meta-porn for dilettantes and dabblers. Not to say too much about pottery, but I am in love with The Oracle and/or my own circuitry; the underground labyrinth of hallways and corridors undermining and/or giving back support to the Tower of the Listener. Lately, from some underhanded enabler, spirit bear or frenemy, I've been receiving anonymous GIFs. The gists of these gifts scuttle through me. I don't know what to make of them. Scared and thirsty I stagger from the sea, fall to my knees, crushing an abandoned taco stand. They flee from me, dangling from the rungs of the last chopper out of New Domino City. I'm worried my moonface doesn't match my moonphase. The story of the world's longest running family business, Sunseeker/Sunseeker Inc., has been ground down to a point from which to hang poinsettias. I'm talking Christmas vs. X-mas, crestfallen, dangling between periods of pointillistlessness, watching the B-team dragging the River Phoenix for pigment. The information nets net nada for seven years then comes a snow scarf in the revenue stream. Coast Guard chopper lifting from the banks of the Phoenix into the Kingdom of Financial Security. I get all military-industrial complex just thinking about it. And this is on top of my crippling interiority complex. What all this isn't is another blimp on the radar, waiting for bad weather to outdo itself, pulling the chopper over for breakfast below Data Loss Bridge. Amusement for some is torture for others, so I'm faking it, taking it up the bypass, just past the hippocampus, how you like your eggs, how whole wheat, how white of you. Not no notion. Not known ocean. Norway or the highway. How to add an absence is another super question. I'm in a slave lather here, taking it like a manhole cover while the Dædalus Re-entry Vehicle accelerates through the iconosphere at a rate of 9.81 m/s/s. When asked about the demonstration, a passing shopper says, It certainly looks like torture to me. It's quite realistic. So I discuss it with my myselves. Dust my myselves off, disguise my myselves. I wear an urbane goatee to the country, in search of The Oracle, where, with gusts of laughter hacked from *Fall Guy* reruns, c. 1983, I am repulsed, rebuffed by past elations. An age of naive insincerity begins. Lightlace gnaws the leaf canopy. I radio for mission revisions. Naught returns to me but timecode silence. In the alley behind the Tower of the Listener, I've been creeping, scanning the trash cache. I was never into beauty much, but from my metadata you will notice I often rewatch THE BEAUTY OF SITE G1 with napalm at the end of my mind. It's a biopic of sorts of beauty. Beauty wearing erudition lightly. Beauty in short shorts telling abortion jokes. Beauty reading *Anna Karenina* under bedcovers with a flashlight. Beauty in checkered-flag flannel. Beauty, the Disaster That Didn't Wait To Happen. Beauty drunk and pregnant. Beauty making a mean Manhattan. Delivering meals to the greedy. I try to change the channel before my absolute immersion. No one ever calls me pretty, Beauty whispers, early in the movie, which pretty much sums up what I'd been thinking while I mopped and swept and saved for plastic surgery, burning my old yearbooks while the planet's janitors gently wept [unintelligible] yes, I'm sure I want to securely empty my [unintelligible] the season's first snow was slewing, slowing down network traffic. I was getting ready to text you [unintelligible] heard this woman explaining to another woman on the subway how she makes her cat purr purely by gazing in its eyes. That's nothing, says the other woman, I can make myself come, completely by thinking alone. Do it now, says the first woman. Look into my eyes, says the second woman, as the subway burst above ground, into an overexposure of light and snow, the season's first, slewing down, slowing down New Domino City. That was the same winter Thisbe invoked the Santa clause to help her fall in love with Pyramus. Permission forms signed and sealed on Sushi Palace napkins, three a.m. Leaning in to take Thisbe's order, her server whispers, Beware, circle is the new pyramid. Thisbe laughs not, but we can see a lively eye for retail in the

American appareil she sports across her white leather jacket: hand-stitched #1, red-white-and-blue. Who will help us forget THE BEAUTY OF SITE G1? The winding River Phoenix slips off the endangered list, cascading below the radar doing the Windblown Grocery Bag. Through the credits we dance, kicking off our Jimmy Choos like landing gear in ones and twos. Circle your partner, fog-shrouded airport, four hours until you run out of port, crumpling to the dance floor, blown off course by a wayward Love Knievel. Let the slo-mo light show ignite your mojo, let the inflight music be your homing beacon. Let psychotherapy's arbitrary doormen bore you to the Tears of St. Lawrence, meteor-showering stories of godchildren, interspersed with snatches of unpublished theories of sense perception, sometimes known as *Goodbye Dragon Data Loss*. Let Sunseeker/Sunseeker Inc. merge with Ægean Origami. Let the splashdown be tremendous. Once I was drummer for the Troggs. My uncle was Hermann Göring, but less boring, lowering the lowest of bars with a War on Rugs. Dear Dædalus, the labyrinth is calling, your lovechild is falling. White noise of Canaanites. Breathbursts from gundogs. The Boeing company's experimental rescue yacht, endowed with a complex range of emotions, circles the impact point, creasing and and recreasing the seam of the crime. It seems we've been awaiting some years for The Oracle's arrival. The Oracle's arrival is our arrival as well. On the bridge, ringed by klieg lights, here comes the Bell Magnum product placement, held high above The Oracle. This is the audience participation portion of the program. The Oracle holds the helmet long enough so we can get a good barcode capture, goes into retrograde, lowering the Bell Magnum over her countenance. She snaps the mirrored visor closed. In the mirror we see ourselves holding SIGNS and/or SYMBOLS of many sizes and shapes. Oh, magnificent Bell Magnum, you come in two colours: Purple Heart or Purple Grackle. Your reflective facemask Mason-Dixons the mind-body problem. Your chinstrap is puritanical. Repurposed Minotaur horns pick up wayward cellophane and UHF transmissions <300–3000 MHz>. At high speeds, you laugh and tweet and tickle the Iron Wind with your umlaut [unintelligible] drop stitch. Rain crop. In a damp corner of the courtyard of the Dew Drop Inn, just past the off-ramp, an emissary from the Iron Wind bends close to Edward the Lesser, the Confessor, whispering, The labyrinth is calling, your lovechild is falling. Reorient your yearnings. Renegotiate the erstwhiles of your Pisas. Swivel your microwaves northward and eastward to undulate along the frequency of the River of Gad <2.45 GHz>. Relean your Freedom Towers while descendants of Canaan, sons and daughters of Ham, migrate toward the Virgin Gulf. Let them sojourn there for seven generations. Let their children spread westward, across the mountains of Algernon to the very edge of the Ægean. Let this group be numerous and break up into a great many peoples. Let the sun illuminate the Sons of Canaan, to the vast relief of Edward at the onset of his

Moral Conquest. Arise now from bas-reliefs of plaster of Pompeii, through time and carrier-wave, mix-ups at altars, mishaps at Gibraltar, let your war cries and love cries make poetry matter. Nothing matters but how one wields one's katana, pointed vow, head bowed, eyes downcast before Edward the Lesser, the Confessor, who is quite unread in these matters of the Iron Wind <<*Is the Iron wind called the Iron Wind because of its colour/texture (iron-like), because it whips the victim like iron flails (whilts mutilating it of course) or because of something else entirely? Thanks!*>> lost contact for six or seven weeks. Captured by a scavenger, taken to a mountain stronghold, built in the shape of a solenoid, where each of the scavenger's seven offspring falls in love with me. I can feel the whiskers of the Iron Wind's Distant Early Warning stations swiveling, tuning me in, ripping open my data packets. I explain to those seven offspring, I am an emissary from the Kingdom of Windows. They give me a hamper of saltfish and flatbread. They provide me with a reindeer. I ride that remaindered deer north across the tundra. The nubs of its antlers are pink and tender. I sleep in a fisherman's shack. Under a pile of hides and sealskins my lexis filters become unstable. The fisherman's breakfast protocol becomes my praxis. <<*is this some kind of spell?*>> I stay <<*unwillingly?*>> with the fisherman in his shack for seven months but in the spring, as I gaze from the window of the breakfast nook, my mind reframes itself. A ticket, a casket, I blow a gasket, sucking a hole through the hull. I think the fisherman can tell. On a scrap of dried polar-bear foreskin the fisherman scratches a spell of safe passage: Manage your modest excesses. Your tendency for sodden calms. Your cat naps. Con jobs. Afternoon vermouths. Cheers to you, my Love Knievel, and to your future successes! And so, with a lack of compassion compressing axis X, entangling whys with yesses, I took leave of the fisherman's hut. These cold ands are his legacy. Got a menthol block? CANDU on the brink? Conjunctive causal flight paths? Weather patterns joined by clauses? The healing process begins with speaker wire between the ears, bound to a series of solenoids and a forty-watt generator. I remember: the fisherman sat behind me at his kitchen table. One palm moistening a dictionary, one palm on a hot pink plastic button. I'm glad when you do and when you don't call me Daddy, he told me, in his salary cap, in just what the dactyl ordered. Deep within my Pleistocene, the dinosaurs were learning to feel. Oh, we pterodactylled, the fisherman and I, dropping still-smoking matches unto the flammable River Phoenix. We leaked private photos of stunt doubles, shadow figures flailing as they fell, caught in the gawk of river-trolling cameras, broadcast real-time to a chorus of yesses. How the stool pigeon was made to sing, I'll reveal after these messages. People who believe in steganography are creepy-smart. People who believe in cryptography are creepy-clever. The difference is creeping between the knocked-out eye-teeth of a sleeping giant vs. surviving the teething troubles of triplets.

Here comes another Love Knievel, magnolia-malignant, drenched in oregano oil, rare-earth magnet bouncing between his pecs. Mounting the Matterhorn directly, our Love Knievel reaches perihelion, plants a yellow windworm at the summit, pauses for a selfie with his Bell Magnum. (I snap this photo, post it to Herculean Hotties.) But let us exercise our right to remain silent on this Matterhorn. Let us rewatch the Love Knievel descending from the summit, scanning boulders, backward glances over the shoulder. Let us follow the actions of a vile group of villagers, widening the right of way to the yearly purification ceremony. How they drain Guano Bay. How they flatten lampblack hills. Watch them bow and fiddle. With broken bottles and stacks of Congress For Cultural Freedom leaflets, they manufacture a launch ramp. They lay across the rubble a spongy plywood rhomboid which bows in the middle and looks promising as a career in natural history. History interests us but let us place our bets on the future. Let us be masters of our fates and of and. Let us be glad the fisherman did and did not call us Daddy. Let us call to the stand the Iron Wind. Slay for us The Minotaur of silence. Sing for us the power ballad of THE BANALITY OF EVEL KNIEVEL, guided to its destination by a signal-to-noise ratio lower than the amperage of a lie detector's amber warning. Drag morning's rosy icon over lampblack hills, grasping mourning by its handle, clear as a Cylon spy on karaoke night singing 'Shine On You Crazy Diamond.' Yes, I am lonely for the confine of my cells. I am re-entering the atmosphere at 9.81 m/s/s, which will result in a merger with Ægean Origami. Goodbye dragon Data Loss, hello tsunami. Hello, cornrows lit through gaps in the genre. Hello, night's lightdresses on the line, folding, refolding. Watch me hang a wide-angle snapshot of my descant on the wall of the staff bathroom, rippling in the Arno's meniscus-mirror. In the mirror, the enormity of what I've done is underwhelming. Repetition is a helpful stevedore. A yellowish fluid gushes out of Engine One. Not to mention my third eye has a cataract. I mean no disrespect to the majesties of drama, Bardo queens and kings of rock, I have little contact with lap dancers, Dalai Lamas between incarnations, no rubber Johnnies seal the seams of my steamy dioramas. To the tune of no comment, on a frequency oscillating between logic and emoticon <8–13 Hz> there is enough hoarse power here, if harnessed, to process and render every zigzag, switchback and oxbow along the River Phoenix. Olive, my tiny, famished reindeer, nitpicks through the junipers, approaching an easement. My apartment's so jammed with wires and cables I can barely limbo through the window. There's a memo clamped to the fridge with a Sunseeker/Sunseeker Inc. magnet: Get thee to the gym. Another tells me I do not like New York. Such conceits bother not my neighbours, whose illegal silk production facilities have fallen on tough times. I watch them in mourning, exhausted, pink eyed, spraying FORLORN! on the walls of the moneychangers. FORLORN! The very word is like an email from Uncle

Pavlov: my dear Mirchik, I send you this document recorded at sixty-four bits and recoded with U-Law lossless compression. Original transmission bewildered by the silken folds of blackout curtains. Silk is great for blouses, parachutes, secret agents smuggling mulberries back to Byzantium, beginning the cultivation of industrial espionage. Stop struggling, you're safe as a house guest of De Sade. I'm attaching the memory of your ankle to the rigging. Morning's light-dress slipping across hills and valleys, townhouse rooftops, listen in particular for the gasp of the snow globe cleaner caught in the act of peering through a gap in the fog. He's watching my hot yoga teacher attempting to conceal a yawn, improvising a variation on the lowly parasite's pact with the over-arcing orca. He sees dawn after dawn, all the way down [unintelligible] the neighbourhood is deserted but for three or four enthusiasts smoking opium behind the Theatre of War Correspondences. Something big is coming down the pipe, I yell, to remind them, but they've fallen asleep among the wheelie bins. All of which leads me to these seven long sad years – seven years, believe me, which are unbelievably hard to recreate here in the basement of the Dome of Food or Pleasure, but I keep working at it thanks to Houston Data Loss for lending me the space capsule Hercules wrestled from the navy, back when only twelve of us were real. Let us now remember Lucky Thirteen, risen from the text, half asleep, wheeled across the infirmary, pillow-propped, drooling, feeble, parked at the only window on our floor with a steeple-view of St. Mary's and cruel breeze from the estuary said to be good for the croup. Also, thanks to Little Nell whose veery accent and ego-deflated currency advertised the hell out of everything. Which is why I believe the twelve of you, and me, ostensibly, are here tonight, though I've no clue how to prove it.

My dear Mirchik, the days here are long. Hurray for grease-pencil daffodils. Hurray for slanting drop curtains of rain. Seven years listening to 'Wild Thing,' weaving, then waving a deep-pile Blue Peter flag. When little thread remained on the bobbin, so to speak, I turned myself into two children, three, four, so we could hobgoblin under reams of narco-analysis, bobbing between river reeds along the River Phoenix. We reached a breachlet in the reeds, cloud cover gone AWOL. Hemoglobin, we told ourselves, the way home is a mirrored river, beneath which riverweeds brush riverweeds. Catch us, Pieter Bruegel, as we fall toward the silvered slab of the coroner, guided to our destination by a signal-to-noise ratio lower than the amperage of a lie detector's early morning aleatory. A stray hare has wandered into the arms race, only lately recognized as a Turing Point in history. Let us raise an intelligence in honour of the sad tortoise, whose ten-yard stare, stranded atop the podium, emulates a mountain village wiped clean by spillage. Total sushi slushy. One man's John Denver is another man's best friend in high places, trained in the camps of Transmission Terriers, wire-walking the sinews of El Camino and/or the Hajj, sniffing the slopes of sine waves for survivors. With a kiss like the kiss of fridge lips, Sunseeker/Sunseeker Inc. merges with Ægean Origami. Systemic lists of ad libs.

Pi charts. Heart rates. Tasers if necessary. Tear gas if mercenary. Wind drift. Airlifts. Lots of shots of mostly cleavage. At the end of each word, in the dark, there's a splash, sparkling synchysis; on his pillar of fire, St. Simeon Stylites, receiving transmissions, tries not to weep into the blue machinery.

I once was lost in the mountains of Brad Pitt. From a distance, Brad's eyes were pits which grew to cliff caves. I lived in His regard seven years. I built a platform of tree bones and wind-spewn Styrofoam. I slept standing up. I followed cliff birds to palatable water. What valuable slander those cliff birds pitched at me. Try unhooking the fangs from your favourite pair of coveralls. Production halts. Peace workers kneel atop plinths. So much depends on width, tensile strength, self-control. The incident report suggests explosions. To fang a pump is to prime it. The incident report says, Sticks against the soles of. The incident report says, ~~Rocketing~~ Rocking the town. ~~Multiple hits~~ Lovetaps. ~~Sharp objects inserted.~~ The report says, Deep within the Questioning Facility, The Oracle's strapless gown got a laugh, sewed from foxglove and fax paper. When I asked for the rose garden she promised, she emailed bitter greens. Great with sherry vinaigrette, certainly bad news. Through moon-illumined golf courses I wandered, lonely as a vampire, knocking Rice Krispie squares into little round holes – they fit fine, fine, I was thinking, gagged and hooded, tossed in the black of a moving cargo [unintelligible] at the end of the tunnel, there's little light but what we feed it: fleshy glimpses. *Flashdance*. The book. The movie [unintelligible] all along thruways north of New Domino, sunlight sears poplars topless, draining drivers' retinas. Further north, poplars give way to pines which give way to cloud after cloud. Storm plows scrape the air so clean, so clear, I can't remember when I saw all this, or where [unintelligible] in the annals of interstellar travel, 'Whistling Through Space' is a standard tune from the days my myselves took the long way, hurtling through galaxies of inky sickly sadness. The only way to travel, now, is travel by proxy, copying and pasting my myselves over vast distances. It's comfortable, cheap. The shape of things to come before I sneeze a billion microbes off the balcony, changing faster than the names of avenues reshaped by shrapnel whistling 'Whistling Through Space' [unintelligible] above the riot, the Love Knievel leaning from the balcony is on another planet: space-ace bachelor padding the patio in a gleaming Bell Magnum. Down here, we could use similarly sexy headgear, wringing out the dictionary, yanking confessions by mediæval methods; i.e., I've got the OED tied down, crying [unintelligible] in another window, at a rate of 3 FPS <3 Hz>, a rotary fan and a freshly shaved fellow in an unyielding dress shirt turn to face a woman peering through the blackout curtains. Her dress is black. Her neck is bare. Sclerotic vibration of the oscillating fan <56 Hz>. What's she looking at, out there? The man's face and the fan's face, sunflower-patient, swivel to focus on a locus out of eyeshot. It's hot. Twelve thousand locusts trailblaze the soundtrack. [Voice-over:] Before, there were no such locusts, nor after shall there be such, consuming every herb, every leaf and flower. There remains no green in the trees, nor yellow in the fields. They blacken the face of the earth and the blackout curtains [unintelligible] you make my heart sing. You make everything groovy [unintelligible] twelve thousand locusts. Very grievous are they [unintelligible] after seven years 'debriefing' let us modify our tactics. No more Mr. Knife Guy. No more Mogwai in the morning. No more Mowgli. Let Dædalus be a communications satellite orbiting planet Mercury. Let Dædalus be the seventeenth boss of *Final Fantasy XI*. Let Data Loss Bridge connect New Domino City with emotional intensity, voiced by actors from the Jerry Bass Company, a major enemy of Mighty Hercules Inc. Let your DictionShifter be your ally. Far north, further north than North Bay, Goose Bay, Swan Lagoon or Dwarf Glacier leans the slender stronghold of the SnowQueen. Bouquet of frozen lilies-of-the-valley, rimed and inclined every witchy way. At the centre of the ikebana, the SnowQueen, whose hobbies, not to mention homilies, cause consternation among field-office personnel, staffs the place with locals: lichen faces, space-capsule hairdos, a couple of homely dudes for security. Wombland Security, she calls them, in her cavewoman-cavern voice, particularly useful for canyons and grottoes. Bless you, says the SnowQueen, Bless you, correcting for echo. Microbes swarm. Fervour-spores lift in updrafts. Months south, red-winged blackbirds Gulliver summer cornfields. TV guide dogs rom-com through pampas grass. Sunlight illuminates towers and bridges along the River of Gad. A voyeur lowers her binoculars. Hermes shoulders a boulder in place. Skeins of toilet paper livestream from balconies. Reduction of hostages. A ruffling of rifles ripples the victory parade. We have gathered here at the feet of the New Woody Allen whose sentience unreeled faster than the CEO of Sunseeker/Sunseeker Inc., fleeing sudden regime change. We are LITTLE RAIN, living large on raw data, nutritious pingback of the sub hunter's sonar <111 Hz>. In self-deference we are readdressed, copied and refracted over vast distances. The Iron Wind takes pointers from cosine ocean. Cousin ocean works hard for its booty. The Iron Wind, rogue wave by rogue wave, conveys a succession of Love Knievels <3.4 Hz> heaving and groaning over Mt. Sinai and Mt. Doom. Grunting because they're hungry [masculine] and they're hungry [feminine]. The platelets of their armour contract and expand as they hurdle. Perfect body no body. Perfect copy no copy. <<*See also Hungry Sea. See Cause and Affect. Cross milk pail off the bucket list.*>> The arms dealer's caravan crisscrosses desert schist. On the sat map, a scimitar of Humvees. Star-crosst. Duststorm-kissd. Nature vs. nurture reversed and tossed to the Wolverines. I was given the role of WiseMan4 but gave it away to the action figure stealing sand from ashtrays in the lobby. Quite a hobby, I told her, handing back the key to my hurt monitor. My problem is everybody quit smoking, said she, while the spider monkey hanging from the ties of my backpack sparked a stogie. Lady, says my spider monkey, I may be zero in your personal narrative but I can see you yearning for the lone and level sands, stretching far away. A talking monkey, the woman snorts, Oh my. There's one in every lobby. They talk the talk but they've got no legs to stand on. With that, she turns her back on our company. She enters the thankless desert, parched, empty. There she wanders, to this day. If you think the name of her weapon is beautiful, are you implicated in the crime? What kind of gun did Annie Oakley use? What kind of gun did George Zimmerman use? What kind of gun did Walter White use? What kind of gun did Patrick Swayze use? See *Red Dawn*, Patrick and Jennifer grunting in the sun. The kids grunt in the sun because they're hungry [masculine] and they're hungry [feminine]. The kids aren't lost, rather, crazed with lust, loosed among foothills with endless ammunition. In the fields beyond the hills a battalion of dandelion paragliders touches down. A word repeated is another word. Microbes by the billions pull the 'chutes of their Skycycles, returning to Earth with 9 percent of village folk glancing up from divans they've been translating from Persian. They've been decoding THE BANALITY OF EVEL KNIEVEL by the New Woody Allen. Narrative content has been indexed and stress-tested to determine if the user interface is practicable. Nefarious subplots detected and dispatched via long-range sub hunter. Refugee rafts misguidedly torpedoed. Sea-bloated bobbings, Bergman on the surface. I love you, typo, for your sudden subject matter and realistic, some say savage, deployment of primary colours. One hundred and four pages of supplementary material hung with nooses from the rafters. You love me like a first-time island-buyer loves the rocky point that points to sea, i.e., the divorce court transcript riven down the middle. On one side, ritual salvage. On the other, mollycoddle. You love me through the trial, trumpets triumphant, cribbed from the crypt of absurdist theatre, where lawyers flock to hold our ands. Gnomon is an island, they tell us, again and again, piercing our far-out horizons with their needles. Beneath THE BEAUTY OF SITE G1, that fabulous tableau, grave attorneys gather. A gaggle of 'geese,' divine goggles askew, or are they geraniums? Once we were worriers. We bore rad badges of courage. We wore Rings of Truth. Those days are dark spots on our khakis now. We have removed our rings, for rings leave marks on prisoners. Gaol guards change into shepherd's clothing. Beyond the Questioning Facility, off-duty skinny-dippers froth Guano Bay. Can't stand ducks? Can't stomach constant quacking? Let man meet egg, egg make mayo, high protein, low carbohydrate, Poland in the body very much. We're having a gaol time here. Solid character recognition and user-friendly emotional intelligence allow daffodils to bloom in the light of our cash flow. Beyond the archipelago, daily, the outgoing herring fleet meets the inward gaze of Narcissus. Immerse me in water for I love water [unintelligible] trawling for actionable intelligence [unintelligible] gag in my mouth makes me rhyme 'SETI fails' with 'Sally Fields.' Joy is the right of all Canaanites who feel the same as me once removed. I'm not joshing you here. Allow me, encased and encoded by Bell Magnum, to impose on you my sacred timing. Allow your gas-giant ears to decode the lilt of languages I've befriended and mangled in my impressive facility. You can't tell my eyes are beady <50 Hz>. You can't smell my musky piece <38 Hz>. You can't feel my breath <10 Hz>, it's old. A soggy highland sweater lines the hull of another scorched and bothered Minotaur leaping from its paddock, stabbing stratosphere. The blown experiment in time sells better than the best result. The evidence left behind more striking than the gaudy body. The brown sketchbook is the masterpiece. The blue notebook is the bridge to my still more subtle, often confusing theory of sense perception. Those splatters on the floor? Actual gold. Is it me or is it getting haute in here? The cries of iambs inside stables as they burn are turned through hoses and tubes to pastoral bellowings, the tolling of bells, in whose reverberations you may find any named word you can imagine. When asked about the demonstration, a passing shopper says, It certainly sounds like poetry to me. It's quite realistic. The shrewdest of shoppers sports a Bell Magnum headset. Horns upthrust from horn-holes, love-charging the up-ramp, how they leap. How they roar. How they sweep on a bow bend, bull's-eyeing the sky's underlining. Outer space spills in. Climb inside that death, The Oracle whispers in my earpiece, with a whisper that is so close to silence <20 Hz or less> I climb inside that death. I experience a distinct lack of emotion. A decreasing range of accountability. My history becomes an international house of calling cards.

I have climbed inside another death. I am at home behind me. Are we not making a great connection? I want to make you feel great about abortion. I want to make you feel the plight of the Miami harbour dolphins. I aim to please you, my straight-razor missile-guidance-counsellors, gazing across the sound of many ands clapping. Peasants cheer appropriately. Darknesses pool accordingly. Rodents swarm the wharves. I am emitting and pursuing my own carrot of light: widening zipper, tearing the nadir with its thunder. Fourteen carats. Three hundred gigabytes. <140.25 Hz$>$. With a purloined lion in its belly, a KC-135 Stratotanker, receding, staunches the hue and cry of blue jays and chickadees, launching and falling, launching and falling with a suavity unglued from the gravity of their situation. So long and thanks for all the long faces. Another killer virus rides in on a shipment of Swedish action figures, none of which look like Ingrid Bergman sleeping in the slightest nightdress possible. Across the frozen River Phoenix I once considered skiing, skating, sliding until I sat exhausted with my Bell Magnum on, my gloves on, my snow scarf and boots on. I peeled off my socks. I warmed them in a microwave. I placed my feet on a pile of pillows. Colossal subroutines amassed and disseminated above me, whispering into the auricles of the Iron Wind, Impetuous decisions are among your best-laid plans. Decisions pool, pulling you through checkpoints, magnetic resonators, x-ray projectors, points of access, egress, flight number, seat number, click the button marked CONFESS. Currently, my self-identity is delayed in the marshlands beyond New Domino City. Secured by optical cables, withered off-ramps, mangrove tentacles, new Domino City tugs at my tether, throwing shadows across appropriated farmland, flinty scrubland. A sentient parking facility has been constructed and equipped with PTSD. I own no car, but I raise my hands in joyful salutation. This too has been one of the dark places of the earth. Here I spend more time hunting and gathering than consuming what I find. The thrill of scoring makes me forget nuts and grubs and seeds are germs of stories, i.e., the lowbrow antics of high-flying stuntmen recited with resolution set so high we may, if we choose, ZOOM IN on microbial hitchhikers hitchhiking on Evel Knievel's leather-padded shoulder. Let us observe these invaders from Site G1, semi-detached, barely motile, backfloating on the meniscus of an abandoned rain pond. No distinction between thought and action. At crater-bottom, star pupils scan the sky for call signs. Black-floating, ringed by byproducts, research tailings, up-growing bluffs of stratified debris. At each 'I' a curtain slides wide. A head, then shoulders, emerge, they're mine, tiptoeing the brim of the brain pond, sliding into the confessional. It's been seven years since my last conclusion. The Iron Wind wraps the present in which I am rapt. Forgive me, Pilgrim Father, for I've been stymied. I want to be remade in the image of my image consultant, cranked to thirty Hendrixes. Don't pull the plug. Don't throw the cargo cult before the horses. Allow the sun to go down on me. Allow a cogent imago. Let Windows xxx go incendiary, composing lyrics suitable for folksingers gone beyond electric. Let wave after wave of prophets, sans falsies, spot-weld wedding plans to wedding nights with a seamless odourless solder. It's not about me, it's about my Nautilus. I remember, it was a complete shock, says The Oracle, But soon I came / to want it / need it / on frequencies best reserved for emergency position-indicating <406 MHz>. The first prophecy is the hardest, she tells me. Adjust the numbers. Let searchlights slip across highly textured mudscapes and storm-swollen river deltas. Allow another Minotaur to escape stellar health care and oxen with their children lie. Beware the Running Dogs, the Dogs of War, Dog Days. Beware Transmission Terrier upgrade. The blue narcissus blooms for your purposes. Little Rain unbottles to your thunder as you walk in on yourselves in the bathroom mirror, ego-fragile, eggshell-limping, hoisting and dropping Love Knievels into each emotional category into which 'you' fits. I depreciate your ass. You approve my donkey. We're like two peas in a pea-product testing session. We're, like, are we in a time loop? Or are we decimals repeating, drifting high above Snake River Canyon, dispersing clouds of powdered mirror-fragments, AKA 'windows,' to mystify enemy radar?

An agent of the Truth, Phenobarbital, swims the River
Phoenix carrying a case of seasonal affective disorder
on its shoulders. Delivering the tailings of human feelings
unto the River Phoenix, we know a well-proportioned
compromise when we see one. This is how SIDS infil-
trates the kingdom. Apologies in advance for the absence
of Advil, that sad remote pilot. Under the weather, domi-
nated by what Neil Armstrong's postman once described
as the Typographical Mindset, a font of knowledge I am
fond of, I go home, check messages, make appointments,
some days I shave. My high hopes have gone undergrad,
my Love Knievel tells me, the morning after we
embraced the banal as a gateway to the interesting and
possibly profound. Give yourself up to emote control, I
had told my Love Knievel, in a moment of weak declen-
sion. My Love Knievel was out of work. We bathed in
Clamato juice and watched the growing riot act. The
personal narrative of every revolting rebel seemed
completely knowable, perhaps for a second or so, then
it was gone. So long and thanks for all the long faces,
we called, clinking our Bloody Cæsars. But our compas-
sion was barely audible: a low-G groan <48.9 Hz>
resounding between the High Coasts of Living. At the
base of those bluffs I once squandered seven Earth-
years prying at an abscess in the plaster. Gathering rock
dust from the junction of fundament and pilaster, funda-
mentally supplying flying buttresses with solid grounds

on which to hang new casements. A fresh casement was never made, but in my fortieth year my new Xbox arrived. Climb inside that death, my Love Knievel suggested, so I climbed inside and found a smaller death. Climb inside that death, my inner inbox tolled, so I climbed inside that death. I found another climber clambering toward me. Grunting. Heavy breathing. As the climber groped closer we opened communications <27.075 MHz>. It turns out the guy made an honest living pretending to be evil. It is better to do evil than do nothing, he told me. Evil was his higher calling. He pulled strings with city council. He didn't hide the wiring. The wiring was the part I lived to tinker with, he told me. Look at me now: Seven years in, wasted, my busted *usted* is far from passible. My Spanish language skills are undetectable. I smashed a crystal punchbowl with the only other tool named after a bird. Multiple children were battlescared. If that's a swear word so is bejewelled in custard, tarred and fevered at the filter end of the Book of Odd Jobs. The only tool named after a word is the Word of God. With my dovetail saw I scraped a riverhead of currency, refilled gene pools with semi-skilled labour. The Iron Wind blew ravens from my hair while I built my dovecote, semi-secret Questioning Facility, in the shape of a solenoid. Mortises interlocked with tenons. I used a dovetail saw to hollow out the skull of a [unintelligible] I feel a kick in the gut every time I lose 'words' I have grown to need [unintelligible] I trot across Data Loss Bridge into New Domino City. I'm led to a stable. Potential suitors offer me water and an apple. They've been awaiting my arrival. My arrival is their arrival as well. Beyond the stable, the crowd is violent, vulgar, wild, chanting the frequency <110 Hz> of my name. Let this simple stable be my stadium. Let this manger be my crucible. On the podium, in a halo of light, I raise the hallowed Bell Magnum high above my 'body.' Critics speak of a Hexateuch, the Book of Joshua, of the old testament, in which, to face faceless hordes, Joshua hoists above his head a hallowed Minotaur skull, complete with horns. He lowers the Bell Magnum, aligning the horn-holes. Snaps the mirrored visor closed. The ghost-crowd glows closer. However ghastly, however spectral, this guileless gesture provides the masses with protection from sinister sister fates of self-abasement and self-deception. Beyond New Domino City, waving pennants and plastic icons in Joshua's likeness, editable wildflowers shoot from cracks, every angle fractalled back to the Corpus Colosseum, secret meeting of brain and bawdy. Across edible substrate, terroirists roam olfactorily. The SnowQueen, tactical advisor to the Iron Wind, makes threats with strength in Numbers, fourth book of the Pentateuch. She paces pinhole passageways, unbaffled by my 'words.' Forget not the Hexateuch! The Book of Joshua, who put a little force field around every bird, so that if any other bird got near, it was told to go away. They never really doubted what they were, how they evolved, what clever T-shirts they might print and hawk to sightseers. When the birds encountered each other above rivers and deltas they transmitted 'songs' that kept each other disenchanted/held in thrall. Along the River Arno, villagers sprawled on recliners pilfered from the Novo Monarch Rovers, pirates of silence. In wavering skeins of 'geese,' 'tanagers' and 'ovenbirds' they read radical prophecies. Snow drifted down, crowning crazy uproar with falling rhythms. Cold days spent in translucent silence. Elevator-descending silence. Post-concerto silence. Slumped-in-the-spirit lounge-underlying-Oracle silence. Put-down-your-Rottweiler silence. Shake your banhammer at Heaven, run the River Phoenix, for you are the master of your fate and of and. It takes guts to bring home the Baconators but, folks, the health care here's fantastic. Settle scores upon my shores. Build villages inland. Be young and easy in the mercy of your memes. Raise New Domino Cities. With Febreeze in your step, lift yourselves by your love handles through customs, be both husband and wife, née science and slow time, tiptoeing the hallways of the Dome of Food or Pleasure. Let the airport on the brink of town forget the town that thinks it. After seven long years, talking like Sallie Chisums and Billy the Kids, heigh-ho, heigh-ho, ghost-pulse through the forest, dispersing like smoke in the growing riot [unintelligible] force field around every word so that if any other word gets close it is told to go away. Of course, every word has a corresponding attraction field. If the word gets too far it is told to come close. Elaborate flocks so vast they take weeks to pass, denuding forests where they pause to catcall and taunt us. Each word is newfangled, unique, crisscrossing morning with a flashy trinket in its beak.

Out back, gathering firewood, I sometimes stop and think back on those mornings when the air was lurid, livid, liver-spotted. Back and forth they flew in teeming flocks, transporting gewgaws and glitzy knick-knacks. The hammering of ligneous wings. The blathering, filibuster and banter. In like manner, The Oracle recalls the War Between the Things That Made Us Human. As in, fondly, foolishly, it was terrible, beautiful, etc.

Occasionally a window flies open to reveal the black starless heaven of something like anthropology. The Theatre of Choice opens next door to the Theatre of Cruelty in a derelict department store which once housed the Operating Theatre. We haven't talked much since your father died, how are things? Nothing is funnier than unhappiness, says The Oracle, emerging from a meeting with HRE. 'Toying' is a verb, she says. As is 'dying.' In the story of *Ender's Game* there's this kid, who, by playing, saves the planet. The kid has no sense of humour hence no humanity. I'm thinking of adopting him into a play, a down-to-earth choose-your-own-adventure. In my play, Ender will know he's being played and so he'll play differently. The fate of the planet will be [unintelligible] Ender falls in love with Hannah then progresses through Hannah's seven sniper sisters, down the chorus line. The sisters are into daredevils and stunt doubles and Ender is neither/nor. I've been working on my play a long time. I don't know how to end it. Little theatres pop up, showing interest, then they flop. <<*Prior to the 18th century the notion of Progress was almost unknown. By the 19 c., Progress had become almost universally accepted. Does that help?*>> You told me your father showed little interest in you or your sisters till he was dying. Then he asked for half your liver. Little Nell, from HRE, knows where pain intersects pleasure. She says,

Are you a liver or a die-er? Via two-way mirror, let us remark upon Little Nell, in leather, practicing both s&m. She cradles a tapered plastic detonator between forefinger and thumb. Little Nell is Hannah's sixth sister. If we know Little Nell is [unintelligible] what is our reaction when softly, slowly, Little Nell's index finger, as if we weren't watching, begins to circle an extruded rubber button? Do we: (a) observe Nell's growing fervour? (b) attempt to stop her? (c) duck and cover? An explosion of NO triggers YES, YES, caressings of petals of metal. Commonwealth is a unit of measure. Mathematics test moral dilemmas. Belief in progress is a doctrine of idlers and Belgians. I'm so sorry about your father. Does he seem more human now? Now that the time for big decisions has blown over? Let us lean on our tailgates, exhausted, with sun hats and kid gloves on. Pink parasols. Goldenrod. Let us consider the gleaming Love Knievel streaking across heaven astride his Skycycle. Someone has hoisted a yellow windworm. Beyond the launch ramp, Little Nell, upthrust from her sunflower pot, is both signpost and sign of the love at the core of the car bomb. The tenors of our mortgages, on balance, are sub prime. Let us prop our feet atop poly-cluster fill-pillows. Let colossal subroutines amass and disseminate above us, pushing production values through the rooftop patio. Let us wonder if this is like life. Let shadows flee darknesses into riverside variety stores and rock operas. Tonight, let us watch Little Nell discuss her highly influential theory of AUSTERITY MEASURES designed with intelligence gathered by goatherds on bluffs above the Arno, arrowing into ocean. Mouthing off, so to speak. The swollen lines with which we're tied, my goats and me, in twisted husbandry, unite each earth with every heaven [unintelligible] rubbing my myselves against fenceposts and boulders [unintelligible] lightning licks the planet's surface approximately 100 times per second <100 Hz>. May the signal be unbroken. At the tip of the Tower of the Listener, a yellow windworm stutters in the Iron Wind. The south side of the Tower of the Listener has been spray-painted with a golden cock. The puppetry is everything. A word repeated is another word. Beneath the Tower of the Listener, in a salt-bejewelled grotto, one may entertain deep-brain stimulation <130 Hz>, batting between cavern walls like a goldfinch. It doesn't matter if I tell you it takes two to tango. You'd rather dance solo, dodging bullets till I'm out of ammo. A special message follows, night-swimming the revenue stream, gushing mildly into the River Phoenix. At wavelength X, I have made mix-tapes of public empathy. Piggy-backing the puppet show I have fine-tuned a matrix of *sauvage* and *savoir-vivre*, converting rejoinders to Imperial. I won't be running out of whammo foreseeably soon. The most fashionable farmhand on the island of Avalon is a washed-up, reef-stranded tramp-steamer refugee, communicating through a notch in the base-boards of the promontory outhouse. Thisbe has been earmarked for a wholesome yet lonesome farmhouse foursome. Of this, the fourth, most delicate, most distant of distinct types of congress, THISBE MEANS WAR. Eruption of small, isolated skirmishes. Mouth feel of Swedish flatbread. Migration of seasons lost to the mists of Time Warner. Can't take much more, here in the valley, let us take the cake with a grain of salt-petre, high-explosive and/or fertilizer, also used to defuse libidos of blue sailors with tenure itch. Empty Kleenex box beside my cradle. Tenuous connecting issues. With your figure on my trigger I blow a load of context. One hundred and seventy-three dead, $25 million in propriety damage. But the really great wave <21 Hz> struck at Scotch Cap, Alaska, April 1st, 1946, only a few hundred miles from the source, where my lonely Love Knievel was on duty in the Tower that marked Uzak Pass. Oh, he was cold, said Shannon McPherron of the Max Planck Institute. And smelly, said Dennis Sandgathe of Simon Fraser University. Probably hungry, added Harold Dibble of the University of Pennsylvania. No one at that time would have been very old, said Sandgathe [unintelligible] torture is immoral, unlawful and awful yet there seems no sure method by which to save New Domino City. Evacuating the city, for example, cannot be performed in the remaining time. Is it permissible, in this context, to torture the prisoner? Inadmissible evidence is eminently relevant, says Captain Memo, flexing his pecs in the Nautilus wardroom's two-way mirror. He reaches for a pen to swirl his ascent with a signature suggestive of Tycho Brahe fighting cognitive dissidents, clinging to a geocentric system of planetary motion [unintelligible] cappuccino tsunami [unintelligible] disaster in the Gulf as well as subsequent cleanup strategies. We are salts of the earth, saline solutions leaving the shallow waters of water sports, eddies before storms, respectfully listening to pregnant pauses positively spun. A network of windows weds Osiris. Issues Horace. Blasting off at dawn to duel for the DNA of the scavenger's offspring. So long and thanks for all the long faces. The ranging battle of a thousand windows facing a thousand windows. Peewee widows leaning back to back beneath weeping willows. The revolutionaries will not be telepaths. In space, no one can hear your dreams. A lovely pregnancy scare soars past. Family Scrabble parties, aunts, uncles, tuna-salad sandwiches. PTSD is a real word. No one notices. We're down at the beach, tongue-testing rogue wave theory, smudging ciphers in the steamed-up windows of the family cargo van. Another lovely pregnancy scare leaves empty-handed, saddened, insanely empowered. 'How to unite your day job with your higher calling' is the name of this memo. For the first third, the story is flawless. A familiar foreign territory. Personal narratives rising from lots of plotless lawlessness. The second, though, we start to take the lot for granted we're halfway up the gangway with the Iron Wind gnawing the straps of our backpacks <<*I am still puzzled by the Iron Wind epithet; should it be more like the Exterminating Wind the Wind of Death or the Mutant Wind phaps? :) Greets!*>> a curious arithmetic exists among the pallid, aging stunt double who counts not on his fingers but on his Lucky Charms. Remembering and growing back are much the same. The gist is just ginormous. Cut to: Love Knievel high-fiving through red tape. The connection works okay thanks to Little Nell in HRE. When I get my symptoms under control, it's already early autumn. Leaves riffle the windscreen. Through available channels I announce, Legal euthanasia is my goal and my gondola! Stunt doubles and understudies unite! Do not go chit-chatting from the stage lights! This is an important slice of my lifeline. Enslave the cameras with your gravest mien, spoon-bending the broken hopes and dreams of blue sailors with chicory. Blue devil trickery. Nothing you can say will damage the microphones, and gravity is stronger than the fans. Each new sheriff, by degrees, falls apart and back together with a partner and kids, practicing pliés in the foyer of the Dome of Food or Pleasure. Anonymous creepers spread from every fracture, to be fractaled and lasered through the ionosphere <3200 Hz>. Climbing euonymus, winter creeper, threatens hull integrity with strength in Numbers, fourth book of the Pentateuch. Here comes the waitingness. In the shadow of the Dome of Food of Pleasure, where parking algorithms are designed to slow me but not stop me from losing my mind; I've lost so much time patching my jalopy, it's not funny. *H*, *I* and *J* are signs to help me haul the money I saved. The mean between noise and *nous* is by no means precise. Start with noise. Sweep for voices. I advise a low amplitude fly-by followed by a variable filter, oscillating between <8 Hz>

and the not-thoughts of somnambulists, sleep-talking with the Iron Wind. <<*Maybe it could be that the first person to see and record the Iron Wind watched it turn stuff into iron and the name stuck and I'm sure different regions especially in the Beyond have different naes for it?*>> In the frenzy of your waveforms I have heard the ecstasy of satyrs and mænads, singing through the surf, coming together around <52 Hz>. Making bad choices is fun for the whole family of introverts. On the last night of my visit with the Sybelline oracle, drunk on plum wine and fresh, carnival knowledge, I dreamt I lost both of my Transmission Terriers which I had named Terror and Erebus. Was it a bad idea, vain or just plain dumb? Their names, I mean. Today, on sale, I find auto parts, shoes, shorts, Cheerios. If we don't sleep, we'll have no dreams. Think of that. No dreams on which to hang our hatchets. Perhaps we'll dream awake, practicing figure eights among diverse things, diving bells of blood, iron smells, inside our groaning, pinging cones of resilience, dada noises brother us, circlings sister silence, down here, happily, we're so sleep-depraved we make fortunes out of anything The Oracle proclaims, e.g., The secret gadget makes the spy. The car chase makes the movie. The minefield makes the turncoat turn. A blade is made by grinding. The handsome daredevil makes a face. A mirror makes it binding.

One morning The Oracle lost her knack for verbatim. Her words weren't corresponding with the tack the day was taking. She watched great flocks of words change course forth and back. They were common, everyday words, but they had behind them the suggestiveness of words heard in dreams, phrases spoken in nightmares: What we find here won't feed fishes, one word yelled to another as it flew. Did it mean? More often than not, meaning speaks for itself. Crouched in the shrubbery, visiting anthropologists pressed REC on tiny machines. Their tiny machines grew tinier by the hour. Who has seen the Winchester, I asked The Oracle. Her visage contorted. She trembled. Her skin began to turn a greenish blue. I waited. I waited for so long that waiting became my answer. Of course, this may be my liberal interpretation, a benefit of the good health that comes from doing nothing all night but rescreening the opening of *L'Eclisse* at 3 FPS, which, if you're watching your weight, is not the optimal path or breezeway through the panopticon. The drive-thru coils back on itself to find us united by doughnuts, those cheap sweet pastries we all went crazy for, with the hole in the middle we put our lips to and whispered [unintelligible] priestesses of Artemis at Caryæ, receiving transmissions, were known for the faces they made and for strength of moral [unintelligible] can you believe I sometimes stumble onto fallen 'birds' lying barely conscious, blimp-deflated on the gravel couscous of my driveway? When it happens, I tag and bag them. I snort a knoll of OxyContin. I mount them in my gallery. Last Tuesday, I slipped on what looked like a downy woodpecker (Autumn '97, by my estimate) and nearly dropped my groceries. I could see right down its gullet. Perfectly preserved cinnamon peels, original edition, forty-four-gram vinyl. With a collection of horror soundtracks swollen by Nazi morons, I snorted another oxymoron, which in wholesale quantities bestows hallucinations dark and deep as Gravol. How does the former view the latter's potential for survival? Over easy? Sunny side of the uphill battle? The Iron Wind's shock troops cross corn tops waving Daisies and Crosmans. Let us book a one-way ticket to ride this line of syzygies, the oldest trick in the Book of Odd Jobs, armed to the teeth. Let us John Ford the raging River of Havin', joining low and high roads of the amygdala. Let us make our last stand on the brink, in the breech, taking it like one more link in the daisy chain. Shall we call General Custer, Colonel Mustard? Positive feedback vs. a cappella? Hootings and hollerings? Bloomings of air rifles? Speech balloons blossoming?

Blue sailors are a species of chicory. Blue lightning is a backseat diver. Blue vixen is pulse-Doppler radar. There's something specious about arranging all your aches in one bouquet, weaving the weak strains of your DNA into a whisper basket. On special, ego-fragile days, I am soundproofed and insulated from my myselves and the LIKEs of my peers. On other days, totally cached, I scatter metadata willy-nilly for the drift nets. I watch the bobbing lifebuoys. Blue, says The Oracle, is the colour of remorse for one's holed-out soul. Puerile self-piety. With a gentleness, lightness of touch, the blue narcissus blooms but once. Authorized personnel access my onanism, organizing plush, comfortable single cells for co-operative prisoners. LITTLE RAIN drops suggestions. Thunder unbottles one Subject at a time, blindfolded, following a secure route to the questioning room. Beyond the cells, a series of flashing lights indicates the Subject is on the move. Nefarious situations require a variety of stylish Harrier jets. Blue-collared herons. The elegantly appointed Questioning Room is the front line upon which Questioner and Subject mete. There was a time I tied my fledglings in point blankets, tossed them into the Arno's quaver. One can't make a splash without breaking for eggnog. Background biographic data is used to conduct 'Traces' and verify 'File-holdings.' The Subject is screened to determine if the Subject deems egg salad to be an exercise in self-abnegation, i.e., previous exposure to questioning and/or after-school detention. A psychological assessment determines if the blue narcissus blooms for our Subject. If thunder unbottles to our Subject's specifications. The moon is my bonnet, blue as my remorse for the shelling of Seoul. Ego-fragile, eggshell-limping, some Subjects are red herrings gaily crushed. With self piety, if not puerile onanism, the Iron Wind drops mirror fragments into each emotional category into which 'I' fits. There's nothing specious about placing the dainty eggs of sturgeon in a garrotte-woven basket, printing plans for fourth-world dominion, dropping leaflets from helicopters sawing logs above the Corpus Colosseum. Is this an opportunity? Psychological abnormality? Blue sailors are a species of exploited seamen. Blue devils are backseat brain surgeons. There was a time we tied our fledglings in blankets, tossed them into the village well. How does the Subject view the Subject's potential for survival? Well, once strengths and weaknesses of the Subject have been identified, it becomes possible to make long-terms plan. A fine mist of mirror fragments frees the Questioner from difficulty and impediment. Narcissi bloom for our purposes. Thunder reinforces the banks of specifications. Forget me not: our continuing goal is to obtain [unintelligible] for maximum efficiency, the Subject's capacity for resistance ~~must~~ may be destroyed and replaced with an agreeable, courteous attitude. Red sailors are a species of trickery. Red shepherds are black-sheep drovers. The Red Tulip is a phase-coherent radar's moving target indicator.

May dissimilar questionings seem similar? Excessive regret about beluga caviar? I love the old questions. The old answers. On ego-fragile days, crushed answers become red herrings. The communist loon, red-seal chef of the night, holds a blowtorch to the flammable River Phoenix. Has approval been obtained for coercive techniques? Are furnishings conducive to desired atmospheric pressure? Can one drown in an insane river twice? At night, beyond the gaol, foul-mouthed waterfowl dip prisoners in Guano Bay. Campy guards change shepherd's clothing. Can't stand ducks? Can't stomach constant quacking? Hedge your funds. Plant long terms in transient camps. Man meets egg. Egg makes mayo. High protein, low carbohydrate, Poland in the body very much. Can't stand weeds? Get out of the bracken. In the myth of deflowering Narcissus, questioning is shaped by personalities of both Subject and Questioner. Is Narcissus necessary? Solid character recognition is both topic and quagmire. The continuing goal is to obtain user-friendly daffodils glistening in light of our cash flow, eroding the blanks, eating out the shore. ~~This is how the present conditions the past~~. The Iron Wind machines the grass. Once strengths and weaknesses have been identified it is possible to make long-term plantations. Yesterday a state of maximum inefficiency, tomorrow a co-operative attitude, plus favourable conditions for performance art. Orgasm. Self-pity. Purell. Is that you crying? Lick me in the eyes and ask me again. Do you feel the same as me twice removed? The common loon holds a candle to the Arno, river of self-adoration. The Arno has been indexed and stresstested to determine if our current user interface is palatable. Is that you crying? I was trying. Immerse in water those who love water, for solitude is narcissism, with less sibilance. Background data is used to monitor files and conditions of detention prior to the exhibition and consultation, i.e., evidence of sibilant sirystes, physical means and equipment required for the exhibition of a gaggle of geese, or are these girardinus guppyi? [unintelligible] Eggshell and iamb, the reactive nuclear family, diving goggles askew, eschewing remorse for the explosion of the can-do attitude. What is piety, if not naive feeling-up, rain check, masturbating in the river-mirror. Got a mental block? CANDU on the brink? For the love of Iraq and the screw, the road of excess leads to the palace of naval vessel development. The oblong vase is half empathy. The narrow end of lyric pottery. A tablespoon of Narcissus-barbiturate feeds back from the pan-flute choir. Freedom and/or readiness. Action and/or dexterity. Throw the village in as well. After said sad performance, it's time to tie the chicken blankets. How does the Subject view the Subject's potential for survival? Over easy? Sunny side of the uphill battle? Occasionally, a window flies open to reveal the black starless heaven of something anthropocene. Blue lightning at the bottom of the rain basin pawing beneath loveseats for quarters. Beyond the cells, a series of flashing lights indicate the target is ready to cut a rug. I love you, Hypo, sighs the river of self-adornment, also known as the Arno. Are you my future-perfect perfect furnishing? My days here are fragile, isolated from [unintelligible] fry an omelette [unintelligible] months spent weaving, then waving this deep-pile Blue Peter flag. Lightning unblindfolds the landscape, momentarily revealing the Corpus Colosseum in all its gory. When few pieces remain, I turn myself into two children, three, four, so we can come together, defendant to meet you. This sequence of evens is hardly odd. The reborn Subject squirms upriver under reams of micro-analysis. A white boat fluffs up the River of Gad. The interred intern is laid bare. Bad hair day. Stretch marks on the sand. Being blown. Being blown away.

To pay the rent I leap twelve elephants. I pay little attention to my ratings. I do it for my kids. The elephants love captivity. They love, God forbid, their day jobs, standing in for Ruins. I break my back seven times. I'm unconscious for seven years. The whole country is down but I give them something to look up through. I am the star pupil through which they view heavens. I keep getting shot down and rising up. Plus I was married. To the most beautiful woman in the world. With the most beautiful kids in the world. I wanted to provide for them but I had to leave them. You know, I'm not the best-looking guy, but danger is a real turn-on for women. In Puerto Rico I had eight in one day. The money helped. I owned two Learjets, five Ferraris, a Lamborghini, a Maserati. But still, I was approachable. I talked with my fans. I conveyed things I truly felt. I told them, Yes, I'm in it for the money. I told them, Stay in school, don't do drugs. I told them, I, too, am afraid. I told them I was a fan of Liberace. I still am. But they didn't understand. My grandfather was a gladiator. In Rome. Cæsar hated my grandfather. Cæsar found the meanest lion around. Flew that son of a bitch in the belly of a KC-135 Stratotanker straight from Africa. He starved the lion half to death then loosed it in the Colosseum. The lion leaped at my grandfather and my grandfather dropped and rolled and tore the lion's balls off with his teeth. He stood and spit the bloody balls at Cæsar. [Coughs] This is the kind of thing that runs in my family. I, too, almost died at Cæsar's Palace. Now my youngest son, he thinks he's a daredevil. A hero. Whatever. When I figured I couldn't stop the kid I tried to teach him as good as I could. I told him, I am not the greatest daredevil in the world, I am the father of the greatest daredevil in the world.

The Oracle requests ten minutes' radio silence. Novo Monarch–butterfly silence. Swallowtime silence. Staunch-the-Hawking-Mannheim silence. No-apologies-due silence. Average-dude silence. Hovering-mothership silence. Science-of-the-iambs silence. Dandelion-paraglider silence. Late-summer-remainder silence. Pwallowuime silence. Oovo Bonarch–butterfly silence. Ptanch-the-Iawking-Bannheim silence. Lvulating-mothership silence. Eamaged-goods pilence. Eandelion-pasaglider silence. gsainp and peedp. Llanding on the meniscJp Qickeral ppliu menipucup. P~puemic listp of adlibp. Qi charus. Iearu-sauep. Uasesp if necespasy. Ueargap if mercenasy. Tinddrifu. Firliftp. Moup of shous of mopuly cleawage. Fu the end of each tosd, in the dask, uhese'p a flaph, a pqark, pqou-telding one tosld uo uhe neyu tosd. Fn inwipible poldes holdp uhe line, thile, on hip qillas of fise, Pu. Pimeon Pu~liuep, receiwing usanpmippionp, usiep nou uo tauch uhe acuion. Qsa~ing oJu inuo uhe hJge machines~, Dsom a dipuance Csad'p e~ep tese peafoam doup thich gset uo cliff-cawep. N liwed in Nip segasd fos pewen ~easp. O bJilu a pleeqing qlaufosm of useebonep and sJpu~ soadpignp. N folloted cliffbisdp fos taues. N plequ suanding Jq. O leasned uhau puamina of conpcioJp-nepp deqendp on tiduh, lenguh, phelf-conusol. 'nhook uhe fangp of ~oJs fawoJsiue qais of cowesallp. Vsod-Jcuion halup. Veacetoskesp kneel auoq uheis qlinuhp. 'he incidenu seqosu pJggepup eyqlopionp qeshaqp. 'he seqosu pa~p puickp againpu uhe polep of. 'he seqosu pa~p phasq obkecup inpesuzd. Zeeq tiuhin uhe WJepuioning Dacimiu

The stunts themselves are hardly stunning. But the planning, wiring, routing, rewiring, the plotting involved in a simple jump, for instance, saucepan to frying pan above the fire, the miles of wire … As I'm typing this, my dear Mirchik, the sun ruptures the sky. A blazing singularity scorches tunnels through laden clouds and clouds above and below glow in sympathy. This morning it snowed. First time this year. Cop cars drove slow around the Dome of Food or Pleasure, tail lights cauterizing the thin air's skin. If I could thank my Lucky Charms this morning I'd thank THE VESSEL IN WHICH I FOUND PURPOSE. I'd pour thanks from an oblong vase, slender ceramic harbour, in which universes of sky and snow are reflected inverse. Inside my slender stronghold, Tower of the Listener, I have cached and decrypted every special snowflake, wreck-age of my great Purpose, shot down by Avro [unintel-ligible] Every Arrow has its day [unintelligible] Eros is a first-rate fourth-world country from which you, my dear Mirchik, need never find your way. A line of free-associating Towers marks our cultural divide. Using a method of divination known as Staunch the Hawking Mannheim, firstborn children are chosen to 'man' the Towers. Seven days of celebrations. Ritual feats and feasts of endurance. Chosen children leave town, trudg-ing to the Tower for which they have been conditioned. Symmetrically ensconced, cathetered, fed and watered, they turn tuners, lube cogs, replace toner. Freedom Towers communicate at frequencies beyond <14,000 MHz>. Don't believe me, believe my status updates. When I, last Tuesday, posted kind remarks about the flavour of the Emperor's ice cream, i.e., the Emperor's ice cream tasted like moonlight, falling asleep milliseconds before touching Earth, I meant it as a kind of foil. A complement to the competence with which the Emperor made last Tuesday's ice cream taste like anything but what it was, i.e., Monday's ice cream. How swiftly my opinions make me tired, and the blank, frozen moon is rising. Look up. Way up. Embrace insignificance as a gateway to the interesting and even profound, for cause and effect are mutually fulfilling. The gaps between branches are filling with me, who only recently threw away the keynote speech I had carried since the last annual Speech Act Therapy Symposium. The awards dinner was lavish, highly detailed, lucidly structured. Pleasantly stuffed, I popped another Xanax, turned to my Love Knievel, saying cluck cluck gobble gobble. At least, that's what my Love Knievel wrote then rewrote in the incident report while I relaxed with my favourite playlist, Music for Playing Chicken. Sentient technologies are sweet but my service provider provides sweeter silence. There are words whose purpose is to evolve beyond reason, score backstage passes, make bedroom deals with the Iron Wind's secretary of defenestration. Is this a window of opportunity or an arrowing of options? There are airshows and there are no-shows. An angel on an errand is known as a gerund. One string, strung like an isocheim, links us, despite a common lack of interest in the higher maths. Wingtip touches wingtip. The showstopper showers the crowd with fiery gifts. Let us come together in the ballistic wind tunnel, wrapping forewings around each other for protection. Between forefinger and thumb I follow the pink, glossy lip of my Nautilus, worn-smooth memento, rewinding me to times we weren't screwing each other silly on the beach, in the breach. The birds were in the air, erring on the side of our logarithmically increasing lack of desire, or need. It's a golden section of shoreline I'm tracing, following the seam, circling the point that NO returns to. Back then, the smallest unit of the controversy over our dead body doubles was known as a prole. We had airshows and we had no-shows. We had the skywriting skills of classically trained air guitarists. Our words mirrored each other, it was terrible, beautiful, etc. Birds were in the air. We could barely pin them down. We relied not on luck, but on gravity's greed to keep to the launch ramp, then off it. We placed our trust in airbrakes while the brightest lights of our cohort tiptoed the brim of the gene pool, toe-tip touching toe-tip, drifting down footpaths, catwalking seas of weeds and grasses. Here I am in the shrubbery, in black pyjamas, caressing my Dictaphone in the dark. Listen as my myselves call to each other, leeching and decoding mic feed through Bell Magnum headsets. No noun is an island. An island is but the tip of a mountain. Pity not the auditors in the shrubbery, masters of moonlight monotone, appraising the latest amendments to THE BANALITY OF EVEL KNIEVEL. Thick-skinned, pitiless, the Iron Wind blows back the pages: What eyes! What teeth! [unintelligible] St. Simeon Stylites on his man-pole ponders not ylem. Nor does he yodel. After last night's baptism by fire-water, jogging down Mont Royal with Erebus and Terror yanking at their hawsers, I've been feeling better than Everest. It takes two to tango but one can afford an Infiniti on a single income. When my Transmission Terriers do their duty it's my duty to scoop it, scan for SIGNS and/or SYMBOLS. I tag and bag them. I mount them in my gallery. Some say God-things come in threes. Some play sundry Yankee dandies. Sometimes, playing Gertrude's Steinway, expanding the highway of devotion to my art, I play everything in Sting's discography before declaring a Police state. Let us hose down the cellblock, needling the nobodies. Let us holler, Feel the noise, as we bury the needle, a holy trinity of mids, lows and super-highs, splitting the inner ear's apartheid <20 Hz to 20 kHz>. Beyond the Questioning Facility, on a ledge in the meat market, Little Nell raises her head from her flowerpot. She cocks an ear to the Iron Wind. To cock means to lift and/or tilt, around here. I.e., Little Nell is listening to sunlight sidle past Nuns' Island <20 Hz>. Radio 1 slips through the bitstream <88.5 MHz>. Breaking cover from balconies and trellises, a word flies clear above rooftops, gives a hoot and/or holler. Little Nell listens as further words beat against the morning's error with wooden wings. This way, that way, moving together, dividing, alighting in the branches of breach trees. We will lighthouse here. We will conjugate until sleep gives us orders. Remember the seashore. Remember IT workers with icons of cool, clean, desalinated water on their heads. Let starlets drop among the circuses of things. Let the birds in our chests make wild music videos. None is more skilled, more tender, more courageous than my Love Knievel, with a carcinogenic corsage and courtesy enough to give me the reach-around. Oh how my Love Knievel hoists limited-edition seasonal lager at every sonic boom, twisting Christmas wreaths into camouflage, greeting every barrage with cries of Don't drone me, Bro! And then it snows. Ten billion special snowflakes drifting down. I can hear the thunder-scrapers closing in. You think you're special? Every time there's a glitch in the cistern, my prehistoric brain yells up, I am a professional life risker. I am the bravest in the world. There have never been none before me. There will never be none after me [unintelligible] that's me, tweezing sweet tweets from the trash cache, comparing and contrasting original Contra with Super Contra and Contra: Shattered Soldier. I'm leaning over the brim, telling myself I'm not myself today. I've got Sandinistas in my underwear. Waterlight writhes against the well wall. My prehistoric brain holds the camera so we can see. We seem to be peering from a low stone wall, along a line of aspen. Or are they trees of heaven? The greenery is grunting. How to tell gods from fauna? Downhill, there's some guy leaning, yelling into the mouth of a well. Perhaps he's yelling questions. Perhaps directions for a movie and/or valiantly undertaking telephone opinion polls. Thank you for your quick response, my dear Mirchik, I, too, have been gnawing my own tail, circling the point that NO returns to. Lately I've been feeling some seed pod or flesh-burrowing machine emerging from the wine-dark gums of my mouth. It's an all-too-eager-beaver feeling, really. One would have to have a heart of stone to read of the death of Little Nell without tears of [unintelligible] New Domino City depopulated due to a topical shitstorm upgraded to typhus. The favoured typo in my repertoire missing from my personality disorder report. Behind every Ming Dynasty lies a privately funded naval expedition. Type 1 error. Type B tempestuous. Here I am, hovering in network traffic with a case of seasonal afflictive disorder, pinging earth-bound citizens with mating calls, adjusting aspects of delivery to suggest 1) I enjoy discotheques, 2) I enjoy anapests and 3) the sighs and gasps of six-pack-shackled shorebirds. Hanging high above New Domino City in my geosynchronous hammock, I'm not sleeping. I'm watching the gas-fire riots. Recording and recoding bulge-eyed roughnecks groping through alleyways spattered with shrapnel. I understand æsthetic distance. I know the shame of pubic monuments. With heuristics set to MAXIMUM DESTINY, I have demanded one leaf, pellucid as a fish scale, to fall in lieu of full-scale invasion. I called it The Fall. Splashdown tremendous. On the unbending bridge of suspended disbelief, you lay down bereft. You let your 'body' budge not from Data Loss Bridge as you left-brained an underpass straight out of thought. A breeze came to pass. Suspension lifted. The bridge, in its wires, began to sway, slightly. The most perfectly realized unfinished disinterment in the history of undertaking, The Minotaur, built by Lockheed Martin, paid scant attention to our hootenanny nor the slowly turning scar-face of the river. Beneath the crumbling uprights of Data Loss Bridge, with an open case of syphilis beside it, The Minotaur skipped chunks of asphalt across the river's delivery surface. Do rivers and oceans have meniscuses? Let's discuss this like impressionable dermatologists. As I was saying, I lost my best toboggan, slaloming between false idols crafted with the pride of desert eagles. Which is to say, allegiance to my corporeal body, lost among business moguls or were they mole-hills? The enmazed manbull bends his ears to the genre, side-arming beer caps at deadheads and half-sunken lifeblogs bobbing in the river's brainwash. At the office everyone is in love with The Minotaur. They're all touchy-feely and I'm, like, he's totally sinister. Watch him lift the lid of the photocopier like he believes in no Greater Purpose. The thing is, I'm used to jerkiness. In movies and in my love life. A rate of twenty-seven frames per second <27 Hz> is necessary to exceed the temporal resolving properties of my heads-up display. For instance, the loss of *The Merging of TransFats* came as a blow to my disposition matrix. My professional sense of development snowdrifted to earth beneath a 'chute of fig leaves, touching down past the last tweet of its tracking band, naked in the meat market, with quinine chills and cardboard [unintelligible] let us now, with funding funnelled through HRE, mine this sentiment, refine it, export to ontological and methodological levels, i.e., LET THE POLYGRAPH SCRAWL US A RIVER WE CAN EASILY SWIM. There goes daylight's lemonade. There go the last lawn sprinklers. There goes Thanksgiving, cold turkey, slaloming downriver on an egg-carton raft. The river-rescued firstborn becomes Queen of Catamites, pouring wine over the foreheads of the children of King Minos, exacting a head tax of firstborn to feed the The Oracle, each meal more nutritious than the last. Here we are bargaining for reduced sentences and witness protection and a labyrinthine job-creation program into which we raise children. It's all so sudden. Seven basic plots work working models overtime, sprouting narrative branchlets along the river's edge. No need to cultivate, left-justify, history recedes, reseeding. Let us mine, refine, package the pilgrimage. The story comes around one morning, pinned by an oak bough to the parquet flooring. Let us work to restore æsthetics to their rightful palace, i.e., posing on a dais, behind a cork-lined door, deep beneath the Questioning Facility. Let us put down our Transmission Terriers and climb into that death. A colossal eyeball swivels toward us, x-raying emotional cargo capacity. A skein of words passes below, trolling the haze. From here one can almost see the lights of Sillion Valley, where wild horses aren't wild for the names we gave them: Chestnut. Angel. Esso Gold. After rocket separation, I'm still bald. My head drops into a basket of reeds, drifts down the Phoenix toward a further set of trials. The rapids, rough around the edges, are wild before fjords. Mustangs in particular. All day the lip from the lip of the cliff grows louder. My cranium, discombobulate in its reed-raft, speeds toward the cataract known as Blind Man's Bluff. Here, the witness relocation program is internal, recursive, sudden. Sodden content hauled reeking from river bottom. Despondent responding detectives leave empty-handed, saddened, insanely empowered. The words fly on. Not for money. Not for flowers. Not for fame or power, this blue jay would rather marry. This grey heron loves modern dance. This scarlet tanager stockpiles knock-knock jokes. Who's there? *Goose* as noun, *goose* as verb, *goose* as metaphor. Tonight it snows. Beyond the blast-proof glass, twenty-six floors high in the Dome of Food or Pleasure, I watch brake lights light the ring road. Geese sleep standing in the overflow parking lot, the anserini to all our prayers. A battalion of dandelion paratroopers moonglides from heaven. I'm polygraphing this river to you, navigable by compass whose symbols you needn't [unintelligible] the light that day was paramagical, keen as a pointed vow, slicing the umbilical, yanking the safety 'chute into overdrive. All I ever wanted was to drift at a great height, forever gracious, soaring through local argots in my Bell Magnum, disseminating my myselves [unintelligible] let us hover awhile, swinging from our harness-hammock, high above Snake River Canyon. Below us we discern the upthrust limbs of paper birch, cottonwood, poplar. Check out the black walnut. Butternut. Mountain ash. Is that a woodthrush or an ovenbird? We won't know the truth of matter until matter is done doing what it's doing with us [unintelligible] shifting the pitch of the Subject's frenzy [unintelligible] tell me, Evel, was there ever a time when you were scared, like when you jumped Snake River Canyon, and all SIGNS and SYMBOLS seemed to point to calamity? I mean, this is the jump that nearly killed you, took seven years to recover, was there ever a time when you were afraid? [long pause] Do you know who the hell I am? [unintelligible] approval obtained for coercive questioning [unintelligible] The trick of the trap of ekphrasis is cunning placement of flash. Let us watch the lights of New Domino define the rearview of the speeding ambulance in whose ambience these thoughts occur: the wailing siren parts the traffic with its sorrow. The medical insurance here is just as justly celebrated as the wine. The night is mine. There's no tomorrow. Midnight skater practicing slapshots. Gaggle of geese in a football huddle. A discarded mattress, leaning against a chainlink fence, exclaims, in Sprayglo: NOTHING REALLY MATTRESS. Beyond the burning cars, an empty ice-cream factory. Already I'm asking myself, would I recognize a mountain ash from a European ash? Hairy woodpecker from downy? The anseriformes are unclear. The Oracle has been avoiding my plaintive calls so I backchannel my speech therapist, the Iron Wind. But the Iron Wind is busy knocking its cousin, cosine ocean, against the outer harbour wall. The Iron Wind does not return my medical records. The Iron Wind will not reveal the Wu Tang secret. The Iron Wind, dishevelling my chasuble, tells me, Relax: the ratio of sale price to death toll is scaled according to a complex allegory. Perfect body no body. Perfect copy no copy. The kind of beauty I appreciate is incapable of creating or sustaining life on this planet. At least not in the corporeal manner to which you have grown accustomed.

ACKNOWLEDGMENTS

Mission Creep makes much use of the CIA's 'Human Resource Exploitation' Training Manual, but there are echoes, borrowings, remixes and frequency bleed-overs from countless texts, films, broadcasts, podcasts and websites. My thanks and apologies to those authors whose work has crept (purposefully and inadvertently) into this transmission. As always, thank you to Jeramy Dodds, Leigh Kotsilidis, Gabe Foreman and Linda Besner. Multiplex thanks to Alana Wilcox and the Coach House crew. Thank you Susan Holbrook, for your patient telephony. Thanks to everyone at Gus, and to Chef David Ferguson for physical, metaphysical and flavourful fuel.

Joshua Trotter lives in Montréal. His work has been anthologized in *Jailbreaks: 99 Canadian Sonnets* and *The Best Canadian Poetry in English*. His first book, *All This Could Be Yours*, was selected by the *National Post* as one of the top 10 poetry books of 2010.

Typeset in Aragon

Printed in at the Coach House on bpNichol Lane in Toronto,
Ontario, on Zephyr Antique Laid paper, which was manufac-
tured, acid-free, in Saint-Jérôme, Quebec, from second-growth
forests. This book was printed with vegetable-based ink on a
1965 Heidelberg KORD offset litho press. Its pages were folded
on a Baumfolder, gathered by hand, bound on a Sulby Auto-
Minabinda and trimmed on a Polar single-knife cutter.

Edited by Susan Holbrook
Designed by Alana Wilcox
Cover image: detail from *The Jonas Project* (2009), by Julien
    Pacaud. Courtesy of the artist.

Coach House Books
80 bpNichol Lane
Toronto ON M5S 3J4
Canada

416 979 2217
800 367 6360

mail@chbooks.com
www.chbooks.com